Rainham
and Wennington
Memories

Rainham
and Wennington

Memories

Cecilia Pyke

TEMPUS

Frontispiece: Bill Hockley with his horses, Major and Captain, when Berwick Ponds was farmed by the Curtis brothers.

First published 2005

Tempus Publishing Limited
The Mill, Brimscombe Port,
Stroud, Gloucestershire, GL5 2QG
© Cecilia Pyke, 2005

British Library Cataloguing in Publication Data.
A catalogue record for this book is available from the British Library.

ISBN 0 7524 3671 6

Typesetting and origination by Tempus Publishing Limited
Printed in Great Britain

Contents

Acknowledgements

Every effort has been made to trace copyright holders of old photographs reproduced in this book. My thanks to the *Romford Recorder* for allowing use of the photograph of PC Merrion taken at the Rainham War Memorial, and to Peter Brett for the loan of the Eastwood Avenue photo taken in 1944. Thanks also to the contributors who loaned their photographs so willingly.

Facts have been checked and rechecked but oral history relies on the memory of individuals and memories may differ. I thank again all the contributors for their time, patience and generosity in helping me put their history on record. I'd particularly like to thank Coral Jeffery for her kind support, despite having recently written a book on Rainham herself.

I also thank my husband for his forbearance with my long and continued absences from home or shut away with my computer.

References

Victoria County History of Essex
E.A. Bird
F. Lewis
C. Jeffery

Introduction

Travelling by barge downstream from Barking Reach, the Thames laps the shores and can almost be heard to whisper to the abandoned parts of the marshes that once provided employment and housed families on this, the southernmost part of the London Borough of Havering.

Looking to the left, we pass Frog Island and the site of the old Three Crowns pub, previously named the Ferry Inn. Here, some people drank too much at the end of a long, hard working week; but they had fun too. Before the Second World War the Thames was alive with ships passing on their way to and from the London Docks and a ferry operated from here; but the site is desolate now, overgrown and relegated to the past. Should you listen closely, you can almost hear the laughter of the day-trippers as they relax in the warmth of the sun on 'the beach'.

We pass the old Murex site, the chemical company that employed thousands – many of them local people. Fading murals can be seen on the river wall by the Tilda rice factory and, looking somewhat lonely, the metal sculpture of a deep-sea diver stands in the water, some metres from the shore. A passing barge chugs towards the jetty that is used to ferry waste to the huge landfill site that blocks our view over much of the Rainham and Wennington marshes. Traffic is quieter on the river now and the silence is broken only by an occasional bird that flaps its wings and squawks, disturbing the peace of that section of marsh where birds and other wildlife are now safe in the hands of the RSPB. Serene and lush it joins the Wennington Marsh, then the Aveley Marsh, passing Coldharbour Point with its lighthouse along on the way. And so the Thames flows on, as it has for centuries, to Purfleet, Tilbury, Southend, and out into the Estuary.

The fine buildings and factual history of the area have been well recorded, but this book is about people, and their place in the structure of the villages of Rainham and Wennington which are separated, but closely linked.

Developers build houses but it's the people living in them who form a community. Rainham is the largest village of the two and its territory sprawls north of the A13 (now the A1306) while Wennington, half a mile eastwards, is still a hamlet of less than 200 houses surrounded by marsh and farmland.

Oral history is now recognised as making a vital contribution towards the knowledge of an area's past. Within these pages the community record their memories, some quite recent, but many of a time lost. A time when many people worked on the land and knew their neighbour, offering help in times of illness. Some tell of hardship, but never to receive pity – they seemed a happy bunch, the now-elderly folk of Rainham and Wennington. The marshes provided endless hours of entertainment for the boys, as they searched for driftwood and mushrooms, etc. and swam in the saltings. They spent hours on the dust tips, rummaging among the waste for 'treasure' that could be used or sold on for pocket money. Life for most of the girls seemed more sedate, playing with hoops and five-stones and helping mother with the family, but for some it meant working hard to earn a little money for food. Within these pages you'll read of their lives, recorded as they allowed me into their homes, trusting me with their precious memories. Unfortunately, it's impossible to reach everybody but I've tried to collect a fair representation of the communities within the area.

Life changed with the building of the A13 bypass. New transport links meant more work opportunities, plus the advent of mechanisation meant fewer people were needed to work on the surrounding farms.

The proximity of Hornchurch Aerodrome and the closeness of the river made Rainham and Wennington vulnerable to much bombing during the Second World War, but people seem to have taken it in their stride.

Another generation has now grown up and as times change, their experiences will be different but the old grit remains. There's a great public spirit in Rainham and Wennington. Anything they need, they fight for and if they don't get it, they'll provide it themselves by digging in their heels, campaigning and fundraising. And anything they don't want, like the proliferation of gravel pits and dumping grounds, they'll go into battle against. One can't help but admire such valiant people.

Cecilia Pyke
May 2005

one

When We
Were Young

Sundays in Wennington

I went to Wennington school at first, and later walked to the one in Rainham. There were three children in our family, my brother Howdy, whose real name was Francis Howard, my sister Edna, and myself. All kids went to church in those days and we went twice on Sundays and to Sunday school in the afternoon. Alf Swann was the organist – he ran a coal business – and after morning service he'd collect the rents. My dad was a sidesman [assisting the churchwardens] and I was in the choir – I pumped the organ too. At one point the parson said he thought I should stand down, because I always won the book for regular attendance. We had a Scout troop and a Girl Guide one, and Bill Brazier was the scoutmaster. He lived at No. 6, Marine Cottages and his sister Alice used to take Sunday school – and ring the bell. We weren't allowed to wear long trousers until we were fourteen. After Sunday school, all the boys from the village would go to East Hall farm where we'd play table tennis and were given lemonade.

Stanley Byford

Cowper Road Chapel

I attended the little chapel in Cowper Road. I loved Harvest Festival when they'd have a lovely wheatsheaf and we children would take a bunch of carrots or something like that. After the service the produce would go to the hospital or the elderly.

Muriel Sampson (*née* Ricketts)

Wennington church.

Upminster Road North, 1923.

Saturday evening walk

Dad used to take us for a walk to the Three Crowns for a drink on a Saturday evening and I remember the ditches either side of Ferry Lane. On one side the ditch was black with waste matter from one of the factories and smelled really badly.

Margaret Muscalla

Scrumping

We used to refer to our nearest playing ground, now the Whybridge Estate, as The Pits. It was a vast section of open fields opposite the community centre and, among other things, we'd go scrumping for apples in the gardens of the houses that backed on to it.

Derek Chaproniere

Pumping the organ

My first Sunday school was at the Gospel Hall and for some reason I wasn't overly impressed. I wasn't very old and my friends went to the parish church, so I decided to go there instead. My pals were in the choir and there was also a football team. Since I was keen on playing football – I played for the school – I decided to go with them. My friend invited me to go to a practice evening and see Mr Cook the choirmaster, saying, 'if you join the choir he'll probably let you play for the team'. Well, Cookie, as we called him, heard me singing and after two sessions his words were, 'I'm sorry Bifield, but you're not a very good singer'. I was very disappointed and explained that I'd only joined because I wanted to play football. He thought about it and agreed to let me stay on condition I pumped the church organ. So, I didn't get into the choir but became the organ-pumper, and did get to play football. I also used to be the bell-ringer when I was at Rainham school.

Charlie Bifield

Dennis Payne in his ATC uniform.

Piano lessons

Dad was in the choir at Rainham church and I joined him when I was eight years old. I went to Sunday school there too. I suppose my interest in music was always there and I seemed to read music and play the organ naturally. Mrs Houchell, who lived next door to us in Parsonage Road, would put me right on anything to do with the piano that I didn't know.

Ted Davis

Briscoe Road

My granddad was from the East End and he bought a plot of land in Briscoe Road. He called the little dwelling Ena Lodge and it was quite primitive as it had a septic tank, and he got his water from a well. When grandmother died he sold the little house. When we stayed there we used to play around Berwick Pond and take a jam jar and fishing rod to fish for tiddlers in the stream. I was too frightened to go deep into the wood because my brother said the moorhens would get me, and peck me to death. Briscoe Road wasn't made up in those days and when my grandmother was taken ill they took her to the main road by stretcher because they couldn't get an ambulance up there.

Edna Harris (née Hawes)

ATC

We'd mainly play football and cricket as children, often getting on the train to go to the Thames Board Mills to watch baseball. When I was old enough, in 1944, I joined the ATC which was based in the Rainham school and we'd go to weekend camps at Hornchurch Aerodrome. During those times, I had short flights in an Oxford, a Hanson and a Tiger Moth. While I was in the ATC, we went for a week to Tuddenham airfield in Suffolk and we'd watch about twenty-five planes take off every night. One of our officers was a chap named Reggie Gent and we watched him go into the briefing room on the Tuesday evening, so we knew he'd be flying. We went to see his mother on the Sunday only to be told she'd received a telegram to say he was missing in action. He'd been killed over Belgium and is buried there.

Dennis Payne

Leaving the circus

When we left the circus, Dad decided to set up on his own, teaching boxing and weight-lifting. He was advised to come to Rainham and talk to a chap who owned a lot of land by the Cherry Tree, to see if he could help. There was a big sandpit on the right of Nelson Road and further along, and way at the back, a big farmhouse and we went to live in it. Dad was told he could use the barn to set up his gym and we could live in the farmhouse free; if he would act as caretaker for the land. Nearby was a long lake where we could take a boat out and I recall a round wood they called a spinney where we'd see birds' eggs. My eldest brother was eighteen and he managed to get a job immediately in Self's in Alexandra Road, where they made concrete slabs, so he earned a week's wages. My sister went to work for Thoroughgoods in their farmhouse at Newtons Corner, so there was money coming in from there. Dad set up his gym, and had some leaflets produced by a little printing business in New Road. It wasn't long before the gym took off with the men coming to learn weightlifting and boxing, and the children being taught dancing and acrobatics. We children helped out in the gym too and we always knew what we'd receive for Christmas. It was the same every year – a new skipping rope – as we skipped three times a day, plus a new pair of boxing gloves, because my sister and I had to be sparring partners to other children.

Grace Jones

Holidays in Yarmouth

Dad had a Matchless motorbike with a sidecar – it was mustard yellow and I can remember the registration number – PB4963. He'd take five of us children on holiday to Yarmouth in it, and it was a bit of a squeeze. Mum would be in the sidecar with my younger brother sitting between her feet and one of my sisters and I would be in the dickey seat, with another child on one of our laps. Another sister was in a sort of chair on the pillion. Hubert Road wasn't made up at that time so if it was muddy,

Mum and Dad rode on the motorbike to the Cherry Tree with us children walking in front. Dad was afraid he'd get stuck in the mud, or the springs might break. It took us over five hours to get to Yarmouth where we stayed at the Fowlers' Holiday Camp in Caister. The Fowlers lived in a house where they did bed and breakfast and there was a camping site on the ground, with a little shop and about eight chalets. There were no facilities in those days so Mum cooked in the communal kitchen, bringing breakfast back to us in the chalet. The ground backed on to the Norfolk Broads where Dad would fish for eels. Mum always had a damask tablecloth she took to the beach where we'd have our rolls at lunch time. Later, Dad bought a Morris car and we'd take Gran on holiday with us as well.

Vera Dawson (née Payne)

Youth club

There was a youth club of sorts in Wennington when I was a teenager and I seem to recall it was exclusive to boys. It was organised by the church but since the population was so small, people from Rainham used to come up and join us.

Paul Mudge

'Flood Row'

Unfortunately, our house was the middle one in Bridge Avenue, so got most of the flooding – it was terrible when a bus went by as we'd get another surge of water. At least our house had a solid floor, so we were able to clean up fairly easily and put the mats down again. Of course it was all great fun to us children and we knew it was necessary to take our school clothes upstairs in case they were damaged by water. We'd do this with any of the things that were precious to us. We'd have our bath on a Sunday afternoon and I hated it because it was such a performance. Mum would boil the water in saucepans and tip it into the galvanised bath. I was lucky because I was the first one in so the water was nice and warm but we reckoned the last one came out dirtier than they went in.

We had an outside loo and the bottom plank of the door was missing. Sometimes it would be freezing cold and pitch black when we went outside to use the toilet. We'd go to sit on the loo and our pet chicken, Chester, would fly up in the air, squawking and flapping his wings in a panic. He'd frighten the life out of us and even though he had his own roost at the bottom of the garden, he seemed to prefer sitting on the toilet. Mum did the washing in the sink with a washboard and a bar of soap – she'd get two of us to fold each sheet and twist it, before putting it through the mangle. The sheets were too big for us to deal with really,

so we'd keep dropping them, and laugh our way through wash day. We had no heating so in the winter we used to cut down a tree. The tree wasn't chopped into logs, but Dad would put one end on the fire and gradually push it in further until it finished burning. There'd be half a tree coming out of the fireplace. After that he threw old shoes on – anything so we kept warm. Dad was a labourer but later worked for Murex and he was only forty-nine when he died. Mum worked in the Bell Inn as a cleaner. Through all this, we laughed and were happy. We never went short of food, although a meal was often Spam and mash. We paid our rent to Glenny's and there were times when my parents were unable to find enough money, so the rent collector allowed us to pay a little towards it. I remember him as being very kind and patient. Such an understanding man.

Jenny Scudder (*née* Parker)

'Flood Row', 1983. The houses are almost ready for demolition.

Kay Knight with the pigs.

Little pigs

I'd get £1 a week for pocket money and when my dad bought about five or six pigs, I'd buy the runt. When that was sold, I'd buy another one because my mother and father brought me up to save a little, spend a little. Dad bought the pigs at Romford Market, and when they were big enough he'd take them back to sell them. They were sold for bacon so were never very old – about nine months or so – they get too fat after that, and have to be sold for pork. They'd squeal when they were taken away – I'm sure they knew what was going on. We had a big old copper where we'd boil up the swill, all the old cabbages and potatoes from the greengrocer's shop used to go in it. During the war, if you kept animals, the police came round to check when they were being sold, to make sure you didn't sell any on the black market. I'd spend the money I made from the pigs for holidays and going out. As a teenager I used to go to the Thames Board Mills on Fridays and also down to the Deri Park on a Friday night – for the jiving.

Kay Knight

Cinema

There wasn't much to do for entertainment outside the house when I was a teenager. If we wanted to go to the pictures we could go to the Odeon in Barking or Romford, the Gaumont at Heathway, or if we wanted the ABC, we'd go to the Princess in Dagenham.

Ted Davis

The tally man

There were two tally men who used to come round when our kids were young, one from

Blundell's and another from Craig's. For 10s a week you could buy a new suit, socks, shoes and a shirt.

Peter Smith

Living at Ferry Point

Mum and Dad were married in the 1920s. My mother was Florrie Whitby and I was born in Ferry Lane in May 1930. The midwife was Nurse Chalk who rode on her bicycle all the way down Ferry lane to deliver me. Nurse Chalk also used to inspect our heads at school. Mum was one of the three Whitby sisters, who were named Florrie, Maud and Daisy, with Mum being the eldest and Daisy the youngest. There were also four brothers, my uncles Bill, Tub, Jack, and Reg. My dad had a mop of black hair. The family lived at the farthest end of a row of little houses at Ferry Point, just past the Three Crowns pub. Mum's sister was working for J.C. Field's, the candle factory, when there was an explosion. Mum was taking her sister's lunch in to her that day, and some people found Mum huddled in a corner because she was frightened. Later, she went to work for Field's herself. She'd often row a boat across to Erith – for no particular reason, she just liked a trip across the water. Dad, who was Harry Ricketts, was initially from Camden Town and came to Rainham to find work. He was employed by Murex for a time and later went to Salamon's where he became works foreman by the time he retired. I was only eighteen months old when we moved from Ferry Lane to West Close, off Ingrebourne Road. Before that my mother's elder brothers and sisters walked all the way to Rainham school. My granddad had a wood yard in Rainham and my mother used to take me there to see him. He was known as Old Shaky as he'd been shell-shocked during the First World War.

Muriel Sampson (*née* Ricketts)

Daisy, Maud and Florrie Whitby.

Halldare

Just along from Lenthorpe House, on the opposite side of the road, were three cottages called Halldare but it's been knocked into one house now. We used to call them the BBC cottages because the people who lived in there were named Burton, Bumpstead and Collier.

Peter Gleeson

Silent films

Aunt Annie took us to see a moving picture show being held in a hut in the village. The entrance fee was 3d for her and 1d for us children. We saw the antics of Charlie Chaplin, the Keystone Cops,

Pearl White and *The Perils of Pauline*. There was also a mini-feature starring the cowboy actor, Tom Mix. This was in 1931 so they were silent films with an accompaniment on the piano.

Robert R. Brown

Wonderful life

I had a wonderful childhood, absolutely wonderful, and as kids, we did no damage, just played. One of our activities was to pick up driftwood for the fires – everything was wood-burning. We played on the marshes, picked mushrooms and fished in the streams, not the Ingrebourne, because it was tidal.

Charlie Bifield

Camping

We'd go camping in the woods at The Chase, and go to Beard's the bakers to buy stale cake. I remember there being two people who sold milk – there was Durley's, and a Mr Flint who lived at the end of Cowper Road. I was told Mr Flint had two thumbs on one hand.

Dennis Payne

Night-soil people

I was born in Blewitt's Cottages, near Dovers Corner in 1907. We had an outside toilet and no bathroom so used a galvanised bath in front of the fire every Friday night. There was no flushing water but my people were very particular and would have used disinfectant, so it was never unpleasant. There was an alleyway round the back of us that led to several houses, and the night-soil people used to come round once a week to empty the toilets. The smell was terrible when they were doing it – everybody used to shut their windows. We'd play with our hoops, and whips and tops when we were children, and five-stones,

of course. The Chase was nearby – it was an open space with trees and grass and we'd play there all day. I remember catching tiddlers in the stream.

Vi Watts

Living in Hubert Road

My family came to live in Hubert Road in 1930 and I've lived here on and off ever since. Our father was in charge of shipping for the Blue Star Line so worked from the London Docks. He'd travel to work along the arterial road by motorbike from our house in Grays and decided the journey was too long. Rainham was still very countrified at that time and since it would cut his journey in half, he decided we should relocate here. He bought a plot of land from a market gardener and began building this house, installing central heating as early as 1930. The family continued to live in Grays while my father made do with a little shack in the grounds. We think it had been occupied by the previous owner because it had facilities for making cups of tea… In that way, my father could supervise the building works. We had a lovely garden when we moved in as the plot had been cultivated as a smallholding. Everything grew in rows and there were lots of flowers and bushes bearing such fruits as redcurrants, gooseberries, and white currants. The previous owner also grew rhubarb. Later my father built a tennis court and my brother trained our dog to jump the nets like a racehorse. When the war began Dad dug little plots on the tennis court so he could 'dig for victory'.

Mary Bell

Journey to Rainham

My first visit to Rainham was in 1929 when I was eight years old. My family lived at Laindon and I was invited to stay with

Mary Bell (right) with a cousin, before the Whybridge Estate was re-developed.

my aunt and uncle who kept a shop in Upminster Road South. My grandmother took me on the Southend–London bus which ran along the old arterial road. We diverted at the Halfway House and carried on through Upminster, alighting at Grey Towers in Hornchurch. There we joined another bus which took us through South Hornchurch, into Rainham village.

Robert R. Brown

The 'shoot'

My dad worked on the Cunis 'shoot' for a time, and as kids we'd go down there and get tins of pineapple, all sorts. The rubbish from London came down to Rainham by barge and they off-loaded all manner of things. We had about thirty Christmas trees in our garden that Dad brought home from work. We had a huge

chiffonier in our lounge that was covered in silverware and china – all recovered from the 'shoot' and Dad was able to keep all the neighbours supplied with their knives and forks.

Dennis Payne

Hay carts

I was born at No. 1, Church Lane in 1916 and my brother and sister were born there too. At that time there was no motorised traffic going along Wennington Road, it was all hay-carts. They came down from Aveley on their way to Nanny Goat Common and would call in at Mum's shop on the way. She had a tea shop that was partitioned off so the tables were in the middle – and Mum served mainly big mugs of tea and toast. The shop sold sweets, groceries, cheese, bacon – all the bacon was smoked in those days and I used to help mother bone it out. I had a pasting once for hiding under the counter and eating all the cakes. Later they opened the A13 bypass.

Stanley Byford

Pot herbs

The food nowadays is nothing like when I was a child. My mother would send me with 6d, to buy 2d of mutton or scrag ends, a 1d for pot herbs – that would include the vegetables. I paid 1d for potatoes, 1d for an Oxo cube and another 1d for the pearl barley. She'd make a big stew and there'd be plenty for six of us. I left school in 1922 at the age thirteen. I used to earn some money when I was at school by cleaning doorsteps. I earned 2d for hearth-stoning doorsteps and each set had six steps. I'd earn between 4d and 6d and my mother would give me a ¼d back. You could get plenty of things for a ¼d in those days. On Sunday morning we'd get a pram and go through the alleyways to the watercress beds and pay 6d for a big bundle, then sell it for a penny a bunch.

Dot Barrack

Plenty of space

I still live in the same house where I was born in 1930. We had a very open view around Hubert Road then as there were no houses either side of the large plot my father bought. In fact, two houses have since been built in the space that was on either side of us. Plots of land were being sold in this area for £10 each in the 1920s, and Dad bought two for £20. He built the house himself by working evenings and weekends, and there was no provision at that time for electricity or sewage. Dad worked by a hurricane lamp indoors. We had a cesspool in the garden and Mum cooked on a large coal-fired range called a Kitchener, which also provided our heating

in the winter. Every few weeks Dad would empty the cesspool by pumping the sewage onto the garden – it wasn't too smelly as it was mixed with the water we bathed in, as well as that used for the household washing. I might add that he grew lovely rhubarb. The house was finished in 1926 and Dad was the first occupant in Hubert Road, although the utilities weren't installed until just before the Second World War broke out.

Dennis Payne

Piggy-Poo

We had a pet pig – it belonged to Micky and Jacky Mitchell – but we used to look after it. We'd take it for walks to the clock tower with the dogs and after a time it thought it was a dog, coming to us when we called it. We called it Piggy-Poo and it slept in an old air-raid shelter. It grew to be huge and died in the end. We couldn't eat it. We went out mostly with the Mitchell children along the road. There was a group of five or six of us, with the youngest being about six or seven. To us, the area by White Post Corner was somewhere really good to go – we'd have great fun in the bluebell woods. We were quite safe because we were always together. One day we decided to walk to Southend with some other children. We found an old pram on the way and put the two youngest children in it, so we could push them up Bread and Cheese Hill. We reached Southend though, but caught the train back. Another thing we enjoyed was rummaging on the tip we knew as Black-Jacks. It was along the A13 and guarded by a watchman who terrified us but we'd creep in anyway. We'd find wheels and parts for bicycles – this was just after the war when there were no toys around so we'd go in there to see what we could find.

Jenny Scudder (née Parker)

A rowing boat on the River Thames, c. 1920.

Rowing up the river

When we were living in the pub, I wondered what it was like further up the river so one day borrowed a boat I saw tied up. Going with the tide, I rowed for about a mile-and-a-half up river to Barking Power Station. Then I wondered what it was like on the other side, so rowed across and sat on the bank watching the traffic going up and down the river. I was approached by two security guards because I'd landed on the beach belonging to the Woolwich Arsenal. They took my telephone number and reported me to Mum and Dad, but I didn't get into trouble.

Charlie Bifield

Steam wagons

When I was at the infants' school, steam wagons used to come along the Wennington Road every Thursday. They'd come from Stratford to take the ships' stores down to Tilbury Docks, where all the P&O liners came in – the wagons were run by a firm of ship's chandlers. They used to stop at the brook, throw their hoses in to suck up the water, and go on to Byford's café for their breakfast, before continuing their journey to Tilbury. They'd unload their wares and stop off on the way back for afternoon tea, then return to Stratford. Blue Circle Cement used steam engines as well.

Peter Gleeson

Lemonade

Gran moved from Barking to Blewitt's Cottages at the end of the 1800s and she ran a grocer's shop from there. The shop was the first stop from Barking along the A13 for the cycling clubs en route to Southend, and Mum said they opened so many R. White's bottles of lemonade their fingers used to be sore.

Vera Dawson (*née* Payne)

Rose Cottages

I was born at No. 69, Rose Cottages, opposite Curtis cottages in the Upminster Road South and went to the village school. Further along the road were a couple of houses where Mrs Osborne and a Mrs Shuker sold sweets from their front rooms. They had a counter they stood behind and sold sweets just as if it was a shop. You could get some sweets for as little as a farthing and that was where we spent our pocket money. My granddad used to call in on a Friday night and give us 2d and sweets or chocolate of some sort, so we got some money from him, but also from the washing. My mother took in washing from the Working Men's Club, and she did it for a big old house called The Hollies in Upminster Road South. When the washing was ready we'd put it in a big basket and my brother and I would deliver it. We were given 6d at one place and 2d at another but I can't remember who gave us what. I remember saving up my money and buying my little brother a bucket and spade for 6d. My mother said the family in The Hollies had come over from Canada and the father had an important job in Ford's. They were supposed to be related to Frances Langford, the singer.

Edna Harris (*née* Hawes)

Whybridge farmhouse

I was born in Whybridge farmhouse in Rainham in 1930. My mother and father bought a plot of land on the Rainham Road but had a few problems during construction, so rented a flat in the farmhouse until everything was sorted out. My mother seemed to like moving house so we had several addresses in Rainham and we were living in Hubert Road when I started school in Blacksmiths Lane.

Harry Sampson

Mr and Mrs Hawes with their two eldest children, Daniel and Edna, in the back row and two cousins in the front row.

Mrs Cutmore, Paul Mudge's mother, in Wennington Road, 1952.

Sinking in the sand

Sometimes we'd go to the River Thames by either walking across the marshes if the rifle ranges weren't in use or more usually cycling there via Rainham. A large area had been created next to the Thames on the Rainham marshes to form a type of lake. Here the 'dredgers' that kept the river navigable for the large ships going up to the London Docks would discharge their 'cargo'. When they pumped out the dredgers, the water in the slurry would filter away and leave a sort of mud deposit, which dried and crusted over on the top. One day when I was walking on it with my friends, although the crust looked firm enough, it gave way, so I was left sinking into the soft mud underneath. I went under quite quickly but my friends managed to drag me out with the help of some waste timber that was luckily nearby. I had to jump in a ditch to wash the residue off.

Paul Mudge

Playing in the streets

Unfortunately the Cherry Tree Estate was divided from Rainham village by the A13, which was too busy for us children to cross, so we were unable to take part in village activities. When I was a child I lived in Nelson Road, near the Cherry Tree and our area was very street oriented. We played in the road and were quite safe because my granddad, who lived five doors along, was the only person who owned a car. There was only one hour of children's TV in those days so we'd build camps and play on the waste ground. There were no trees on one side of the road so we used it as a football pitch. Everything we needed was on our doorstep, so there was plenty of street activity. As a teenager I started to learn the drums and a few of us formed a little group. We'd practise in the house and my dad had to sit on the front garden wall because of the noise we made.

Derek Chaproniere

Chopping wood

I heard Mum saying she had no money to buy milk for her tea, so without her knowledge, I found a log and chopped and tied it into bundles of firewood. I took this to Blewitt's Cottages and sold it for 2d a bundle, with the lady in the first house taking three. She told her neighbours about me and they bought the rest of that batch with the result that I had to chop more wood on Sunday to provide the rest of the row. With the money, I bought groceries from the shop at the end of Blewitt's Cottages. I was asked to supply wood regularly and did so for another four years until I left school.

Grace Jones

Rats!

We kids used to earn some pocket money going bean-topping at Willow farm. We'd chop the tops of the plants off so they wouldn't grow too high for pickers to get to the beans. Then there was gleaning. Any peas left on the vines when the pickers had finished, could be taken by the villagers. We'd put them into sacks and were paid so much per sack. For fun, we'd go over to the Cunis 'shoot' and rummage for parts for our bike wheels. My uncle George was a foreman at Cunis and we'd have a swim in the saltings while we were there. We'd also play at killing rats with sticks – the place was full of rats, being a tip. The mud banks were filled with mud that was dredged from London. They cut out squares in the bank and pumped the mud in.

Stanley Byford

Winkle man

The winkle man came on Sundays, when everybody had to find a pin to pick the winkles out of the shells, and then we'd eat them with bread and butter. The muffin man came round on Sundays too, and the cat man with the cat food. If we were out he'd put the food through the letterbox and when we got home the cat would have eaten it. In London, the men off the boats would come round the doors selling materials and the like, from foreign countries. Another thing we did was collect jam jars and the man would give us a ha'penny, or a toy windmill.

Dot Barrack

A parade in Wennington to celebrate the Coronation in 1937.

The tramp

An old tramp used to stop off at Wennington and he'd camp under a tree near The Triangle. If my dad saw him he'd bring him home. He was a smashing old boy, Welsh I think he was, and we used to have a little shed in the back garden where he'd stay sometimes. Dad would offer him a bed for the night but he didn't want it as he preferred to sleep in the shed. Dad took him a cup of tea in the morning and when he'd go back to collect the empty cup, the old chap would be gone. I don't know what happened to him eventually, although rumour had it he came from a wealthy family but he just couldn't stay indoors. Every so often his brother came to find him and try to persuade him to go home, but the old boy wouldn't. He used to talk to us about his travels and fascinated us, because we'd not even been as far as Upminster.

Peter Gleeson

Life in the convent

Dad died of TB and so did my sister, and mum was only earning £1 5s a week in a cork factory, so somebody suggested putting me in a convent at East Grinstead, so that's what happened. It was a C of E convent. My brother was put on the boys' training ship at Grays called the *Arethusa*. I was in the convent for about two years. I cleaned the doorsteps there too, as well as being up at 4.30 a.m. to clean the grates. Every day Sister Maurice gave food supplements to a few of us she thought needed building up. We'd have Scott's Emulsion, cod liver oil and malt, and Parishes Food.

Dot Barrack

Thatched cottages

I was born in 1929 at No. 4, Cowper Road and our house was one of a pair of cottages that were behind the Grays Co-op in Upminster Road South. The roofs were thatched and I can remember birds flying in and out, but whether or not they nested in there, I'm not sure. The Rayments lived next door at No. 2 and there'd be a lovely smell of shaving cream on a Friday night when one of the sons was getting ready to go out. Before he left he'd throw us children the odd coppers in his pocket.

My dad used to keep rabbits – he had hundreds of them of different breeds. There were Flemish Giants with their huge heads, Belgian Hares, Old English ... and he'd sell them to the local butchers. We had gas mantles in the cottage and I'd go with my brothers to get the accumulator recharged – it was used to help power the wireless. We'd buy our sweets from two little shops in Upminster Road South. They were opposite the Co-op and one was run by the Osborne family and the other, the Shukers. Some sweets only cost a farthing. We'd wait for one particular lady to serve as she always threw a few more sweets into the bag. We bought our milk from Flint's at the end of Cowper Road and I remember the man selling mint round the streets.

As children, we'd play cricket on the recreation ground opposite, and more quiet games such as marbles and five-stones. I was an avid collector of cigarette cards and have only recently got rid of my collection. My favourites were the lovely embroidered silk cards that came in the Passing Cloud cigarette packets. They were expensive cigarettes and came in a pink box.

We were flooded out one year, the ground being so low, and the water rose about six feet leaving a tide mark on the walls. I can still recall guns firing on the rifle range, even though I left the village when I was seven years old. I think the cottages were pulled down after we left in 1936.

George Barrett

Thatched cottages in Cowper Road.

Discarded cargoes

Over the back of the houses we used to play football, but in the summer holidays we spent most of our time on the marshes over on the saltings. We'd swim there and when the men finished work on the dust tips, we'd go totting. We'd get copper wire and such like and when the old rag and bone man came round, we'd sell it to him. He'd weigh it up and give us what he thought it was worth, and that was how we made our pocket money. There was a lot of stuff over there. Once there was a ship on the Thames that came from Spain and the London Docks wouldn't accept its cargo of potatoes, so it was off-loaded on the 'shoot' – it would have gone rotten if they'd kept it. People came from miles around to take the big wooden boxes of potatoes home. Another time there was a discarded shipment of bananas. The river was alive with shipping then, up and down to the London Docks. There were heaps of driftwood over there and a lot of it was stillage – they used it to settle the cargo, I think. Once the cargo was off-loaded they'd throw the wood into the river. Nearly all our garden sheds were made from stillage.

Peter Gleeson

Makeshift fishing rods

We played on the farms and around the marshes where we'd climb trees, build dens or play football and cricket on the marshes or on the village green. We'd also go fishing with rods made from a bamboo cane with screw-eyes to thread the line through. The main venue for this was a small pond (rumoured to be an old bomb crater) on the edge of the Thames Board Mills site, on the way to Purfleet.

Paul Mudge

Palm toffee

We'd walk to Rainham and back three times on Sundays, going to morning service, Sunday school and evening service at the Gospel Hall in Cowper Road. We all did that, my parents too. We used to get two pennies for pocket money if we were good, and I used to buy a slab of Palm toffee with mine.

Grace Dalton

Moonlight flit

We were living in Mitcham when we did a moonlight flit. My dad got a horse and cart and we left because we couldn't pay the rent. Dad was quite strict and didn't like to see anybody idle – if he saw me sitting doing nothing he'd tell my mother to give me some sewing.

Dot Barrack

Bubble and squeak

At home, Mondays were always wash days so we'd have the cold meat left over from Sunday with bubble and squeak. Mum would send us to a little shop in a house (with two small basins) and it would be 'a pennyworth of mustard pickle' and 'a pennyworth of pickled onions'. That would be enough for three of us.

Madeline Fatharly

two

School Days

Harvest Festival

At Harvest Festival time, my dad and his brother used to make the wheatsheaf for Wennington church and I'd feel very proud when they brought it into the school which was next door, so we children could see it first.

Ann Waller (*née* Chandler)

Miss Gladys

I was born at No. 2, The Green in Wennington and went to school in the village. Mrs O'Donnell was our teacher in the Wennington school, and there was also Miss Gladys – she was very nice. I moved to Rainham school when I was eleven years old and left at fourteen.

Peter Gleeson

Mr Ward

Mr Ward was a dedicated teacher when I was at Suttons school and on one occasion I came across a sports event taking place at Harrow Lodge Park. I used to love running although I had no proper running shoes, but Mr Ward was officiating and told me to run in my socks, which I did, and won the race. I was given a jigsaw puzzle and a box of chocolates and was so pleased with myself, I ran all the way home again – a distance of about two miles.

George Barrett

100th anniversary

I went to Whybridge school – it was called Blacksmiths Lane school then, and has just celebrated its 100th anniversary. I used to go into Rainham village quite often and remember the people living in Flood Row seemed always to be living in the upstairs of their houses – their children had to take their shoes and socks off, and paddle through the water go to school.

Dennis Payne

RAPS

RAPS, or the Rainham Association of Past Scholars, was started by a boy called Len Scott, probably in the middle or late 1930s. It was for the pupils when they left school. Mr Jones, the English teacher and Mr Daniels, who was the music teacher, took a great interest in it and between them, they got it off the ground. It started off just for boys but later they added a girls' section. They'd have little reviews, a football club, dances, table tennis, swimming, amateur dramatics, and all sorts. They had a National Savings Bank scheme and there was even a yearly newsletter. One Saturday night Len Scott happened to be in London and was interviewed for the radio show *In Town Tonight* and he was able to tell them all about RAPS. Sadly the Association fizzled out as the war got under way but while it was going it was wonderful.

Edna Harris (*née* Hawes)

THE RAINHAM ASSOCIATION OF PAST SCHOLARS

1938
Vol. I. No. IV.

ANNUAL MAGAZINE

The RAPS Annual Magazine, 1938.

Wennington schoolchildren photographed with the wheatsheaf at the Harvest Festival, 1953.

Ball held at the Princess cinema for the Rainham Association of Past Scholars, *c.* 1937.

Two founder members of RAPS. Len Scott, an ex-pupil, on the right and his younger brother in the foreground.

Extra coaching

I didn't go to school until I was ten years old. Since it was my first time they put me with the five-year-olds but I could read and write, so quickly passed up to my proper grade. I had a lovely teacher who stayed behind every night for half an hour to give me extra coaching. In the 1930s there were no houses in the lane where I went to school. It's called Blacksmiths Lane because there was a big barn there with a blacksmith who'd shoe the horses while we stood and watched. My mother had given me money for lunch but there was no provision for cooked meals; I explained it didn't matter because I was an acrobat and, as such, was used to training all day, something that can't

be done on a full stomach. While travelling with Bertram Mills' circus we had porridge for breakfast, and a huge roasted dinner in the evening, making do with milk during the day. However, the teacher gave me a banana from her own lunch pack, and I took my own after that. Discipline in the school was very strict in those days, with teachers shouting, throwing chalk at pupils, caning…

Grace Jones

Fog

I remember the fogs down by the river. The Thames was busy in those days but very few ships moved when it was foggy. There was a lighthouse out at Coldharbour. I remember in 1926-27 there were floods – the river burst its banks and flooded Ferry Lane so we couldn't go to school; just for a day, I think.

Charlie Bifield

Ursuline Convent

My school days started in St Peter's church in Dagenham and when I left the juniors went to the Ursuline Convent in Ilford. We were on holiday in Liverpool when the Second World War broke out and my father decided it would be safer for us to stay there. When Liverpool began to get bombed we went to relations in Ireland then back to Great Cosby, which is just outside Liverpool.

Mary Bell

Woodwork

I went to Rainham school and my most hated lesson was woodwork. I remember messing about and the headmaster caught me throwing wood shavings at my classmates. I was given the stick for that.

Ted Davis

Infants and juniors

I used to go to Miss Swann's infants' school in Rainham village. Miss Swann was the archetypal spinster schoolmistress, but a lovely lady. She lived in a big house with her brother and his wife and she had a school room downstairs, with a music room upstairs that overlooked the clock tower. We only went in the mornings. One day she left all the crayons on the horrible old heater in the schoolroom, and they all melted. Later I went to Wennington school. My mother knew Mr Taylor, the schoolmaster, who lived on Wennington Green. There were only eight of us in the class. The church was next to the school and when there was a funeral we weren't allowed out in case we made a noise. Wennington school was one big school room with a curtain dividing it. To one side was a sink, and the toilets were across the playground, so I remember it as being a bit primitive really. Round the corner was a place we called The Hut, which was the village hall. The infants were taught there, and there were adult toilets.

Frances Painter

Paddling to school

When we lived in Bridge Avenue, sometimes we'd get up in the morning and come down to find water halfway up the stairs, with our chickens floating around the downstairs rooms. We'd put on our Wellies to go downstairs

Coldharbour lighthouse.

before taking down the tin bath that was always hanging outside in the yard. Then we'd be pushed, two at a time, through the water to Bell Corner where we'd put on our shoes and go to school. I can't say how often the houses flooded but it seemed like a lot of the time. Every now and again, we'd notice the water rising in the creek and then sandbags would arrive, but they weren't very effective. We got teased a bit at school as the other children watched us paddle through the water but Mum was always prepared, and everything was stored up high.

Jenny Scudder (*née* Parker)

Children from Wennington

Quite a few children from Wennington came down to Rainham school and lots of women worked on the land because we were surrounded by farms.

Edna Harris (*née* Hawes)

Open-air lessons

I went to the school in The Redberry when I was about four years old and left when I was seven. Miss Swann, the teacher, was very strict. Every morning we had to go outside where there was a big tree with an iron bench round it, and we had to sit on the bench to do our tables. We did that every day, and then we did a few spellings. Sometimes Miss Swann would take us out. We'd go round the driveway, under the railway bridge, scramble up the bank to Rainham Creek, where there were the bones of an old boat in the water. Miss Swann's brother, Henry, was my godfather.

Kay Knight

Secondary school

My secondary schooling was in Hornchurch. I had to get the bus from Wennington to Rainham, then the 165 to Elm Park station, pick up the Underground to Upminster Bridge and walk from there. After a while I used to cycle into Rainham and leave my bike in the paper shop, which was opposite the railway station. The newsagent had a yard at the side of the shop and he charged one penny to leave a bike there for the day. Mainly the railway commuters catching the trains used it. In the summer I'd cycle all the way to school, some seven miles or so.

Paul Mudge

Mulley's

I went to the little private school in The Redberry at first and later attended Palmer's at Grays for a time, but I didn't like it there very much and left when I was about fifteen. Later I cycled to Romford with a friend to learn shorthand and typing at Mulley's commercial school, which was in a house in Eastern Road. If the weather was bad we went on the little green bus to Romford, which cost sixpence at that time.

Ruth Daws

Good attendance

I was born in 1915 and we moved from Rainham to Wennington when I was small. My sister was born there and we went to the village school as our father did before us. Wennington school was next to the parish church. It was a long room with about twenty or thirty children, I think there was Miss Keyes and a Mrs O'Donnell with the latter living at the schoolhouse. When my sister was nine she had to go to the school in Rainham and she used to walk there and back twice every day. It's a mile-and-a-quarter and she had a really good attendance record at Rainham school, losing only a day-and-a-half in four years.

Grace Dalton

Wennington school pupils, 1931.

Coronation party at Wennington school, 1953.

Wennington school pupils, 1950s, with Mr and Mrs Taylor and Miss White in the centre of the group.

Airfield Estate

I went to Whybridge school in Blacksmiths Lane, but due to overcrowding I was moved to a school on the Mungo Park Estate for one year. When I started there in 1956, Spitfires were continuing to land on Hornchurch Aerodrome and then parachute training took over from barrage-balloon training. Later, in 1968, when I worked in the Romford office of Hilbery Chaplin, the estate agents, they had a development office which designed and built the first phase of housing on the Airfield Estate. We applied to have what is now known as Airfield Way called 'Chocksa Way,' but the council wouldn't allow it.

Derek Chaproniere

Wennington school in the fifties

I was about four years old when I moved to Wennington and joined the school when I was five. The infants were taught in the village hall, a large wooden building known locally as The Hut located next to the school building. I seem to remember that heating in the winter was provided by a large coke-burning stove which was on the side wall of the building and enclosed by a large wire mesh fire-guard. We took lessons at tables and chairs placed in a semi-circle. The original structure of The Hut was destroyed by fire in the early sixties and was replaced by a more modern building built by voluntary labour from many that lived in the village. The infants' teacher was Mrs Myall but she retired through ill-health to be replaced by Mrs White. The school was effectively just one big room and the older children were separated from the younger by a curtain across the middle. We did physical exercises a couple of times a week although in summer played an improvised game of cricket in the playground and occasionally the whole school would be taken to play rounders on the village green. A quantity of PE equipment (parallel bars, wooden horses, etc.) was bought by the school and stored in The Hut when not in use. Since it needed to be assembled we weren't able to use it very often. Harvest Festival was a big event at the school. Donations of fruit and vegetables together with tinned produce were made by the parents of the children. These were distributed by the children to the senior residents of the village. Mr Chandler, the baker in Rainham, used to bring the school a large loaf in the shape of a wheatsheaf. This was cut up and given to us at milk time after we had made our deliveries to the senior citizens. Lessons always started with hymns and prayers and progressed to scripture. Sometimes, the scripture lesson dragged on all morning. Some lessons were done in conjunction with school broadcasts on the radio, and during my last couple of years at the school someone from Essex Education would bring films which were shown in The Hut. I think this used to be on a Friday afternoon every three weeks or so. They were mainly educational and sometimes we'd have to do a project about a topic in one of the films. I recall making a model of a lighthouse once as one of these projects. We must have received a good education although it was informal and less structured than current expectations. The school had a good academic record and, looking back, Mr and Mrs Taylor, the headmaster and his wife – who was also a teacher at the school – did wonders with limited resources even by the standards of the day. I passed the 'eleven-plus' exam as did a number of pupils including my elder stepbrother. The school building was converted into a house when the school eventually closed in the late sixties/early seventies.

Paul Mudge

three

Where We Worked

Sector Sergeant

I joined the Metropolitan Police Service when I was twenty-five and served at various London police stations before arriving in Havering in 1986. I was sent to Hornchurch police station, which, at that particular time, covered Upminster and Rainham. In 1992, sector policing was introduced and I became the Sector Sergeant for Rainham and was still stationed at Rainham police station when I retired five years ago. I have a lot of time for Rainham – it's a real community, I remember my years there with great fondness. We used to police all the local events, like the Rainham carnival and the Havering half-marathon, organised by the staff at Chafford school. Great times!

The annual service at the War Memorial in the village draws a lot of people. I'd attend each year to lay a wreath on behalf of the police. Being so well attended I remember we had to close off the roads around the centre of the village. In October 1997 excavation was taking place near Dovers Corner roundabout and a large Second World War German bomb was uncovered. The Army Bomb Disposal Unit was called in to make it safe before it could be taken away. To ensure public safety an exclusion zone of 1,000m had to be established and it was decided to evacuate people from their homes. It was recommended that the families who lived within the zone go and stay with family or friends, if possible. If not, they could go to one of the

ATTENTION

Important Information from
London Borough of Havering
Temporary Evacuation Friday 31 October 1997

A large Second World War bomb has been uncovered close to Dovers Corner roundabout, in Rainham Road (A125). The bomb must be made safe and removed as soon as possible.

To ensure public safety an exclusion zone of 1,000 metres around the device must be established before bomb disposal staff can begin work.

Temporary evacuation of parts of South Hornchurch and Rainham will take place tomorrow morning, Friday 31 October 1997. Your property is within the exclusion zone. Evacuation will start at 7.30am so that the area can be cleared by 8.30am at the latest to enable work to start. You should be able to return to your home early on Friday evening.

WHAT TO DO
It is recommended that you go to family and friends in the surrounding area. If this is not possible arrangements have been made to open a temporary evacuation centre at:

Brittons School, Ford Lane, Rainham.

Council buses will be touring all streets in the area from 7.30am to 8.30am to go to the evacuation centre. If you do not have your own transport go to a major junction where you will be picked up by one of the buses.

A leaflet distributed by the council during the unexploded bomb scare, 1997.

Sgt Gunn outside the police station with the Bomb Disposal Unit, 1997.

temporary evacuation centres. There was one at Brittons school in farm Lane, and another at Sanders Draper school in Hornchurch. It was quite a complex operation and the council provided buses to ferry people about, touring the streets between 7.30 and 8.30 in the morning. Havering Council distributed leaflets telling people to wear warm clothes and to remember to take their medicines, plus food for their babies, and not to leave their pets at home. I remember going to Brittons school to see how things were going and it was like stepping back in time. The spirit of the Blitz had returned to Rainham! Helpers were busy supplying food and drink, and there was a buzz of community spirit with some groups singing old wartime songs – it was wonderful. The A13 was closed off in both directions and instead of the usual thunder of traffic there was an eerie silence. The army was there for about three days and the Bomb Disposal Unit slept in Rainham police station until the bomb was eventually defused and taken away. In July 1995 there was a large demonstration. The community heard there were plans to excavate for gravel in the Wennington Road area and felt so strongly against it they decided to hold a protest march. We closed all the roads in Rainham and used the police helicopter for surveillance, not knowing what to expect really. I think about 2,000 people turned out, and they were all local residents. They had placards and banners, with the march starting from the British Legion Club. The procession went all round Wennington and Rainham eventually dispersing four or five hours later back at the British Legion Club. There was no trouble whatsoever and the plans for the gravel pit were abandoned.

Len Gunn

Becoming an electrician

Dad left the Three Crowns pub in 1936. I didn't want to follow my father into the pub business, in fact I was quite anti-pub, so I studied to become an electrician. I'd observed people having too much to drink … there was a lot of that at weekends. Having decided what I wanted to do, I did my apprenticeship with Roneo in Romford. In 1931 they laid off 15,000 people, which was half the workforce, but they kept me on, I suppose because I didn't earn much money. Eventually I had to go to Murex to learn heavy engineering and it was a good experience for me. I was called up at the beginning of the war and wanted to go in the navy. I had the interview but was told I had to sign on for six years. That length of time filled me with horror so I went into the air force where, ironically, I served abroad for six years. That's justice for you.

Charlie Bifield

The Registrar

I left school at fourteen and went to a private commercial school in Liverpool where I learned shorthand, typing, book-keeping and English. I went to work for the Commercial Union in 1943 and was eighteen by the time we came back to Rainham. I didn't want to travel to the City so began work at the Civic Centre opposite Nanny Goat Common at Becontree Heath, and eventually became a Registrar. I loved working at the Civic Centre

Winter when Hubert Road was surrounded by open spaces. Mary Bell is seen here having fun in the snow.

The old Murex buildings.

– during summer evenings I lived near enough to return there to play tennis.

Mary Bell

Transport manager

I joined the Murex Co. in 1947 and worked for them for some thirty-six years. I lived in Hornchurch at that time and didn't own a car, so used to travel by bicycle or bus. Green Line Coaches operated in Ferry Lane then. The company bought up some of the old cottages down by the river and eventually knocked them down. Providing the weather was good, any employees that wished to would come down along with their families and dig foundations for the various sites needed to house the metallurgical processes. They put in the concrete all ready for the next stage of building. The children were brought along and there was generally some sort of entertainment laid on

for them. They all had their dinners and teas for the day and were paid a modicum of money. Foundation digging was very popular during the summer weekends but unfortunately the lack of piling resulted in the buildings slowly sinking into the marsh. However, it was decided that as the rate of submergence was quite slow, the roof would be raised and a floor built over it, with another roof added. Fortunately, not too many buildings of that type of construction still existed in 1947 and the newer ones were erected on a raft of piles. They went deep enough to penetrate the 'bog', probably some 60ft, then rest on the heavy clay Thames basin. One of the foremen, Frank Tame, was born in one of the houses that Murex bought – those cottages were used as the original works' offices – they still had the old banisters and stairs, whatever. Also, the old Three Crowns pub was quite a landmark and this too was bought by the company and turned into offices.

We didn't find mice and rats a great problem on the site as each department had its own 'mousers' and the marsh itself was patrolled by groups of feral cats and assorted breeds of wild dog, including retired greyhounds. It could certainly get smelly down there, the rich odours originating mostly from the river. It was particularly noticeable in times of drought when no fresh water descended from the Thames' various sources. This would be coupled with 'spring' tides, which are in no way connected to the season of spring, but rather to full and new moons. The latter would cause high and low tides, thus exposing the river-bed and all the debris. Fortunately, this greatly improved over the years but due to lack of dredging, neap tides are now causing contamination as before. Due to these circumstances, we had our 'catastrophes' during my time at Murex. One was where millions of ladybirds descended on us, and we were plagued by blowflies on several occasions. Then there was the spilt crude oil, and the flood which engulfed Canvey Island, failing by a hair's breadth to bring destruction to Murex Ltd. On that occasion I was on site for thirty-six hours non-stop. The river bank has been raised several times since, but with the barriers upstream, the flood tides are just about contained. Personally, working for Murex was a pleasure on most occasions. Henry Green was a gentleman and although he rejected some of my business proposals, he accepted the majority and was pleased with the results.

Ed Kimber

mended. I didn't stay with him for long before I went to work for Murex, then I took a job with Grays Co-op until I went into the army. I was on the bulk-bread vans and we'd deliver bread to the bakers.

Peter Gleeson

In the Phoenix office

I began working for Phoenix Timber (Importers) in 1961. I went there as a temp but stayed for six years, as a shorthand typist. I worked in the transport department and used to drive to work, as I was living in Elm Park at the time. Manor Way was just off the A13 and I parked my car just opposite, in Ambleside Road. The building I worked in was prefabricated and big enough to accommodate large vehicles, although during the day they were all out delivering. I enjoyed working for Phoenix and my job was varied, involving some invoicing, letter writing and filing – I also saw to the post. There were no photocopiers in those days so we made extra copies by using carbon paper. I used to bash away on an old Remington typewriter – nothing like the word processors and computers they use today. We had quite a strict dress code which was a skirt and blouse, although I often wore a suit as I thought it was smarter. There was a partition behind my desk where the drivers collected the dockets they needed for the daily deliveries... I left Phoenix in 1967 because I wanted to work in London, where the money was better.

Betty Hawes

Shoe repairs

I worked for a boot repair man in Rainham when I first left school. His name was Mr Perry and his shop was over the road from the Co-op. I used to go to the houses to collect the shoes, get them ready for him to repair, and take them back when they were

Delins

When I left school at fifteen I worked in Delins which was the first supermarket in Rainham. Later I moved to the head office of Wallis Supermarkets in New Road. They were taken over by Somerfield in 1981.

Jenny Scudder (*née* Parker)

From service to clippie

The nuns at the convent I was sent to were very nice and after a time they found me a position with the Countess of Bedsborough in Victoria. I was a parlour maid and Miss Teal was the housekeeper. The Countess's sister was Lady Raglan and on one occasion, she organised a lovely party at the Dorchester for her servants and asked us along too, as there weren't many of us. I was very happy with the Countess but fancied a change so that was when I went to be a clippie on the trolley buses. My route went from Hammersmith to Clapham.

Dot Barrack

Nursemaid

In the old days you had to take work where you could find it. A cousin of ours who lived on Wennington Green already had several children before she had twins, so I helped her for about a year. I must have been about sixteen when I went to work for the Gunarys – I looked after their children.

Grace Dalton

Boundary Day

My father was stationed at Purfleet during the 1914-18 war, where he served with the Irish Guards. When he was demobbed he was given a job by the War Office on the Purfleet Rifle Ranges, and once a year they used to have what they called Boundary Day. A lot of the people from hereabouts used to work on the old rubbish tips over by the river and in those days the tips were run by Cunis and Corrigan. Workers would cut across the marshes and go over the railway lines, so eventually wore away a footpath. On Boundary Day, the Government used to put a man on each one of those footpaths, just to let people know they could be stopped if the authorities chose.

It probably began with the churches when they used to beat the boundaries in the old days. The church here at Wennington used to do it – they'd begin at the brook, go through East Hall Lane to the New Road, turn right to the Lennard Arms and go back to the church – that would have been the parish boundary.

Peter Gleeson

The Lennard Arms, *c.* 1930.

Clerk-typist

My first job was for Murex in Rainham – it was in the middle of nowhere but I loved it. I worked as a clerk-typist in the post room and thought the supervisor was very strict. There were special wash times when you were supposed to use the toilet and you had your own towels. There was a little area in the front of the building with a big clock that ticked loudly; but only senior staff were allowed to use the front door and the workers had to go round to the back door. We used catch a little bus that ferried the staff to and from Rainham station and paid 3d for a ticket that had 'Murex' printed on it. I loved Friday nights when I'd go to the record shop by the clock tower, with my wages in a little brown envelope. Then I'd go in to Burr's to see what shoes they had. I was with Murex for about four years, then my sight began to fail and I had to retrain. I worked in London after that.

Frances Painter

The Phoenix Hotel

I had a lovely old gran who worked at the Phoenix Hotel for years – we used to say she was head cook and bottle washer, but never knew exactly what she did. She seemed to do the cooking and everything, and would sometimes take me with her and I'd play in the long-room. The Phoenix had a lovely garden.

Vi Watts

On the beat

I joined the police force on 3 April 1967 and retired on 14 August 1997. I did my training at Peal House in London as opposed to Hendon, and my first day on the beat was at Chelsea. Later, I went to Dagenham where I served my probation, after which I went to Upminster as a Temporary Detective Constable. From there I went to Rainham and served in the CID for seven or eight years and although I worked in several areas during that time, Rainham was my base station. Due to changes in policing structure I went to Hornchurch before moving back to Rainham police station permanently, but we'd already bought a house here in 1969. We'd relocated to be near the job and we've seen no reason to move since. Our children have been brought up here and my affection for Rainham runs deep. It's a wonderful community and I have many happy memories of my life 'on the beat'.

We used to run the carnival with two or three home-beat officers who'd make sure they changed their weekly leave so they'd be on duty on the Saturday. That enabled all four of us to be there and we'd ride round on our bikes. We'd get some 'specials' in and a few more policemen from Hornchurch, and organise the whole thing ourselves. We'd go from one junction to another checking all was well. Rainham has always policed itself on these occasions. We had a flood management plan in Rainham, long before the Thames Barrier came into being. We had an itinerary of what we'd do should the Thames flood. One of my little jobs would be to cycle to the Havering Borough Council yard in Upper Rainham Road where a control centre would have been set up. Home-beat officers in those days had to know where all the boats were on their beat, in case of a flood. Then the Thames Barrier came into being and Rainham became part of the flood plain, so Rainham didn't have an itinerary any more. Rainham had a shooting club that used the Ministry of Defence range, once situated in Ferry Lane, and its members met in the Phoenix pub most Sunday mornings. I had to check up on gun licences in the area – small-arms and shot-guns... I knew absolutely nothing about guns, but when I was in doubt I used to go

PC Charles Merrion at the War Memorial.

to see Ivan the barber because what he didn't know about guns wasn't worth knowing. Ivan was a well-known fixture in the Rainham Gun Club. He would take a gun to pieces and show me what the different guns should and shouldn't do. Anything I know about guns I learned from Ivan the barber. At one time we sent some of our Rainham kids to America on a school exchange. Chafford school had a good music department and somehow or the other they got in touch with a school in Carlton, California and they arranged an exchange. We did some fundraising to do it and there were tears along the way. The money was stolen and lots of things went on, but in the end the airlines took the kids on their contingency plan and off they went. I used to like going to work and riding around on my bicycle knowing people knew who I was. People used to knock on my door with their problems for years after I retired. Rainham is so village orientated and such a lovely place to be in.

Charles Merrion

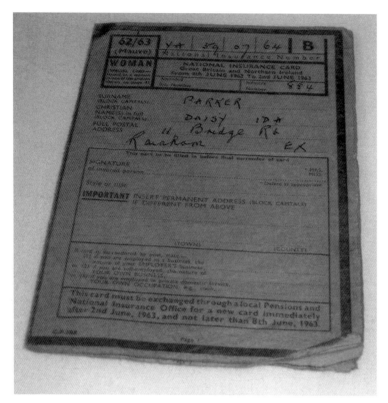

National Insurance card, 1962-63.

No married women

I lost my job when I got married in 1929 as they didn't like married women working in those days – my husband wouldn't let me work anyway.

Vi Watts

The gardener

Dad worked for Murex when he left the War Office, but when Mr Green, who was the managing director, bought Wennington House my dad became his gardener. He was with him for years, until Mr Green left the House and moved over to Shenfield. Dad could have gone with him but he chose to go back to the factory again. I worked for Murex for a while when I left school and I liked it – they were nice people down there. While dad was working for him, Mr Green had a Rolls Royce and

Mrs Green an Armstrong Siddeley. She was very kind to my brother and I, and would take us with her when she went shopping by car.

Peter Gleeson

Floods

When I came home after the war I worked for W.C. French who had a contract for Murex. I was working there when the river Ingrebourne overflowed and all the timber off the Phoenix barges was falling into the water. It came right up to the centre of Rainham.

Peter Smith

Driving for Phoenix

I started work at Murex but was called up for National Service. When I was demobbed I returned there for a while, learning to become

Don Poole, 2004.

a motor mechanic. In 1954 I began work with Phoenix Timber Importers. My job took me to all parts of the country, as far as Pocklington, Grangemouth, Bristol and Liskard. I loved it – and part of my job was to chauffeur the company head about in his Rover car. He was a very pleasant man and easy to work for – he lived somewhere in Kensington. Even though I was his driver, he was unpretentious and I didn't have to wear a uniform. When the war was over, Phoenix imported timber from such countries as Russia, South Africa and Sweden... Phoenix had a saw-mill in Ferry Lane and timber would be taken there from Frog Island where a mulberry harbour was used for unloading the boats. Sadly, they closed the garage down in 1979 and the vehicles were serviced in other areas, so I was made redundant.

Jack Hawes

From Rodenside to Murex

I'd trained to be a fitter at Rodenside Engineering which was on the A13 – just opposite Gale Street. I started with them in 1941 and was there for four years, but it closed down, so I took a job in the tool room at Murex. I worked there for about three months before joining the air force, but returned when I was demobbed. Apparently just before the war our section was involved with tungsten carbide, which is a very hard metal – the next hardest thing to diamonds in fact. Rumour had it that before the war somebody came over from Germany want-ing to buy the powder – tungsten carbide was kept in powder form. When asked what he wanted it for – he drew a bullet on a piece of paper. I stayed at the same place for forty years although Murex sold the tungsten carbide side to BOC who later sold on to

GEC. I was very happy there – it was a company that considered its employees. I recall that, for two years running, they made exceptional profits and without any hesitation gave all the employees a pay rise.

Don Poole

The civil servant

Before I was married I worked at the Central Telegraph Office dealing with telegrams at first, but at the same time went to continuation school and took exams. Then I took my Civil Service exam and went to another branch of the Post Office, training to be a counter clerk and telegraphist. After some time, the Second World War started and I was told they wanted me to go to the Admiralty. We were on a watch system at the Admiralty, the same as the navy, which meant you didn't leave your post until your replacement arrived. The day-watch was from nine in the morning until seven at night and the night-watch was from seven at night until nine in the morning. But, if there'd been any raids and your counterpart was late, you didn't necessarily get away on time. We worked underground in the Admiralty building which was guarded by steel doors with an armed Royal Marine at each one. I was decoding messages from ships and it was extremely interesting. At the end of the war, since we'd all been seconded from other departments, we were given a list of jobs available, or we could stay at the Admiralty. I could have gone back to the Post Office, or apply elsewhere. Some went to the Foreign Office, the air force … and I put down for the Department of Fuel and Power. I was there within two days and the Labour Party had begun nationalising the mines, the gas, the electricity … so it was a very interesting period. I was put in a reception area for a few weeks and then asked if I'd like to go into the Parliamentary Secretary's Office, where I was assistant to Hugh Gaitskell's secretary. Mr Gaitskell was quite a character and a very nice man. I was very busy and had the opportunity to go to the House of Commons and saw Winston Churchill, although I didn't meet him. Mr Gaitskell was later replaced by Lord Robens.

Elizabeth Wiegold

Riding high

At one time, Dad worked for the Phoenix Timber Co. and would go in on Sundays to wash his crane down. He'd take me with him sometimes and let me climb up into the cab. I had a great time, high in the air, pretending to drive it.

Margaret Muscalla

Working with children

I was lost without my husband when he died, and it was suggested I help out at the nursery in the Methodist church in Wennington Road. I was so pleased and I loved the little children, but it was the first time I'd worked since I first married.

Vi Watts

Canteen work

I was about sixteen when my sister and I used to cycle to work down Ferry Lane. We worked about halfway down on the right-hand side. It was a timber firm called Thompson Bayliss & Co., and they made bungalows and things. I was there for about three years, but I think it closed down when I left. Some people said it was taken over by Phoenix, but I'm not sure. I enjoyed it there – I worked in the canteen, serving the workers with their dinners and teas. Some of them used to have their own mugs and when we went round with the tea, we were only allowed to half fill the mugs for a penny. They had to pay 2d for a full mug. Sometimes they pleaded with us, asking for a full mug for a penny, so if nobody was looking, we'd do what they asked. They used to pull our legs – and make us laugh. They'd get proper cooked dinners but always fish on Friday. My sister and I used to cycle to the Heathway on Fridays, to collect the fish before we started work. We didn't cook, only served. They had the rifle range on the marshes, to the left of Ferry Lane. This was before the war, and sometimes the soldiers used the range and would come into our canteen for cups of tea.

Madeline Fatharly

Christian bookshop

I worked in the Christian bookshop in Ludgate Hill for years, and shop work always came first in my heart.

Ellen Dalton

Cold meats

I worked in H.S. Reeve's for about seven years in the 1960s. Mr Reeve was the butcher and I worked on the counter where cold meats were sold.

Ruth Daws

Grays beach

I worked in Reeve's in Rainham for a little while and then I saw the advert in a local paper about a little café at Grays beach that was up for rental, so I decided to take it. I did ham salads for 1s 11d, and a cup of tea for 2d. We did sandwiches and that sort of thing as well. My son used to work at the café when he was on school holidays and he'd serve the ice cream. I think I did well to start a business with £10 – that's all I had, and I made a success of it. I've never been one for sitting around.

Dot Barrack

Madeline Fatharly (left) and her sister, Kathleen (right) with Mrs Scott in the centre, when they worked for Thompson and Bayliss.

Mayhew's/Brigg's Bodies/Murex

When I left school I went to work for Mayhew's, the butchers, in Rainham, then I went to Brigg's Bodies, then on to Murex in their fitting shop. I'd been with Murex for thirty years when they made me redundant, so I took a year off work. After that I went to work for Bailey's, the packing people, then Murex found themselves short of people so asked me to go back. I did, but it wasn't the same without my old mates, so I left again and we sold No. 15, New Cottages in Wennington and moved to Manningtree.

Stanley Byford

The export office

I worked at Murex from the age of fifty-five to sixty and when I had my retirement do I had to have it in the office, as I hadn't been there long enough to have a proper Murex retirement party. But I went back for a few months after I'd officially retired as they needed help. I'd always worked in a shop, and shop work wasn't pensionable in those days, so those few years at Murex gave me a little extra pension. I was in the export office and I really loved it for those last years. It was a good firm to work for, although I found coming from shop work to office work hard at first. I told the boss of my office that I wasn't a typist but on my first day, I was put in front of a typewriter and told to type a chemical analysis sheet – so it was tough. I managed though. I was there when Murex won the Queen's Award for Industry and all the office staff got a key ring.

Ellen Dalton

The lighterman

When Dad was a lighterman at Flower & Everitts, he and his mates used to row to up the river to the Three Crowns for a pint. It was a popular meeting place and I remember some electricians from Murex getting the sack when they were found playing cards there, instead of being at work. Dad worked for Cunis later.

Stanley Byford

Looking for work

I was born in Cressing, a little village outside Braintree and was one of eight children. My father worked for Crittall's, the window people, and they used to put men off at an early age and due to one thing and another, Dad had to go further afield to seek work. Mum packed him some sandwiches and a flask and he cycled forty miles to Ford's in Dagenham, where he was taken on. He'd do the round trip of eighty miles a day on his bike until he was invited to lodge with an old friend in Rainham. He used to cycle home at weekends until he found a house in Stanley Road South.

Peter Smith

Counter clerk

I was asked if I'd like to help out in the post office in Rainham, so I was already working in the post office when the Civil Service opened their examinations to sub-office assistants of up to forty years of age. In that way I became a civil servant and my job became pensionable. I started working in there a week after the Second World War broke out and since post office work was restricted during the war, I didn't have to do war work. The army pensions and air force letters and such like, all had to be dealt with; I had all the lessons in first aid.

Grace Dalton

four

Farms and Smallholdings

The farmer's wife

We'd only been married for three months when we came to Berwick Ponds farm. My husband had been learning the farming business on his uncle's farm in Billericay and we left our little two-up, two-down cottage to move here. You can imagine the change when we took over this eight-bedroomed farm-house. My husband always said we were like two sparrows in a barn. The previous people who lived here were named Curtis. They ran two farms, Berwick Manor and Berwick Ponds – with Geoffrey Curtis living here and his brother, Lawrence, living in Berwick Manor. They had a wonderful milking herd of Friesian cows – they were prize beasts but had to be sold when a gravel-digging company bought some of the land. Although I was newly married, I could cook as both my mother and grandmother were good cooks, and I'd learned at school. There was an old kitchen at the back of the house but it wasn't used. It had an old range and a copper and a bread-oven. We've since renovated that room and now use it for family parties – we had a wonderful party for the Millennium celebrations in there. The newer kitchen, the one we use now, has an electric cooker and is nearer to the centre of the house so more convenient. Years ago it was the main sitting-room because there's a back staircase where the domestic staff had three rooms at the very top, and there was a nursery. We have a series of bell pushes in the house we can use, but these days, nobody answers. We still have the box on the kitchen wall with indicators to show which room requires maid service. The house had been modernised to some extent but we've improved it over the years. It's about 240 years old – the central part was rather tall and narrow, and a two-storey extension was added to either side in about 1904. Apparently the bricks on the outside of the older, central part were red Georgian, but the rooms on either side were built in yellow bricks which were fashionable at the time, so they put a layer of yellow bricks on the older part so they blended in. We used to grow a variety of vegetables on the farm but with mechanisation we now specialise in potatoes, cereals and lots of radishes for the supermarkets. We use the cellar for storing wine as we have refrigeration. Before then it would have been used for meat and other things, as it has a constant temperature. Our son is virtually running the farm now and we only employ two people permanently which is not a lot for just over 1,000 acres, but we have students in the summer to help us when we're busy. We get them from an agency and part of my function is to see their houses are clean and tidy and generally look out for them. We start harvesting potatoes in June when they're bagged up and collected by a potato merchant for delivery to the fish and chip shops in the East End. Our fishing bailiff is very interested in bird life – he identified over fifty species of birds in the Berwick Ponds area from January to March 2003 and he knows their Latin names. There are king-fishers over there, although I've never been lucky enough to see one.

Tessa Fisher

The horses

Dad worked for the farmer, Mr Harry Gunary. He worked with the horses and used to leave home at about eight in the evening to take the goods to market. When I was younger he used to put me on the seat at the front of the cart – it had a little cover that came over it to keep him dry. He had two horses, one was named Bella, and I used to think it was lovely to ride along with Dad. The horses were stopped to be fed and watered along the way and Dad used to say they knew exactly when to stop and exactly when to

Berwick Ponds farmhouse, 2004.

start again. One night he fell asleep and the horses took him all the way home to the farm. When they got older (I was married by this time), Mum and Dad went to live in one of the three cottages on Wennington Hall farm and I used to visit a lot. While Dad worked on the farm, Mum did some work in the Gunary house. Then they were bombed out, so they went to live in another one of Mr Gunary's houses opposite the old sorting office in Rainham, then on The Green for a little while until their house was rebuilt on the main London road.

Vi Watts

Bright's farm

My grandfather had been bailiff at Bright's farm at one time but when I was a child he moved to one of the Swann and Thomson farms at Great Wakering.

Ruth Daws

Land Girls

My wife used to work on the Vellacott's farm – she was in the Land Army. Several of the farms around here used to have Land Girls.

Peter Gleeson

Coldharbour farm

My grandfather, Arthur Blowers, became manager of Coldharbour farm, which was over a mile from Ferry Point. He'd walk along the farm track to the Three Crowns pub to have a drink with his pals. The farm was isolated with just a couple of cottages nearby. When it closed, I think in about 1930, my grandparents went to live at No. 120, Wennington Road.

Margaret Muscalla

Jack Townsend

I was born during the war in the front bedroom at No. 211, Wennington Road and Nurse Chalk was the midwife. At that time, my dad had a smallholding in Wantz Lane. In those days, it was known by the locals as Jack's Lane (rather than Wantz) after my dad who was Jack Townsend. He had a greengrocer's shop at the front of the plot, and at the back he kept ducks, pigs, geese, chicken, rabbits etc., and he used to sell a lot of the poultry to the people in Ingrebourne Road. Dad went to Stratford to buy most of his produce, then he'd go on his greengrocery rounds on Tuesdays, Thursdays and Saturdays. I suppose I'd have been about twelve at the time I began to go on the rounds with him, and when we stopped at the post office in Wennington, I'd buy twelve sticks of hard liquorice. They cost one penny each.

There was a large house where Kent View is now. It had big iron gates and a high brick wall all the way along from where the village hall is, to the row of cottages. I remember a big rockery inside, and a huge walnut tree – I'm sure the house was split into flats at the time we used to go there. In Marine Row there used to be Cutmore's, the grocers, and old Mr Cutmore used to breed canaries. The post office was in Laundry Cottages and was run by Alf Hazell. After I got my liquorice sticks, we'd continue round to The Green, then my dad would go into Church Lane for a pie or piece of cake and a cup of tea, in Byford's café, but I used to go and talk to Mr and Mrs Fitch. Their cottage was very dark inside and I didn't realise until I was grown up that Mr Fitch was the man who looked after the big shire horses. There was a ditch running alongside Lambs Lane and somebody drowned in there, because you had to cross the ditch to get to the properties. Some of the dwellings were like wooden sheds and the people had to walk over a wooden plank to get to them. There was no

Kay Knight with her father, Jack Townsend, on the smallholding in Wantz Lane.

proper road. A Mr Rogers lived there – he used to grow his own tobacco.

Kay Knight

Mr and Mrs Payne

There used to be a lovely couple in Willows farm – Mr and Mrs Payne. If anyone was poorly in the village they'd bring home-made bread, new-laid eggs and potatoes, because if you were off sick then, you didn't get any money.

Peter Smith

Gunary family history

My grandfather, Harry Gunary, ran two farms in conjunction with his brothers, Ernest and Stanley. The farms, Wennington Hall and South Hall, traded under the name of S. Gunary & Sons, in recognition of my great-grandfather, Samuel Gunary, who founded the family business. I believe it began at Marsh farm, Chequers Lane, Dagenham but the land was later taken over by the Ford Motor Co. The farms were mainly arable but pigs were kept at Wennington Hall farm – I believe they were called Essex Saddlebacks and I remember a pig sale being held every year in a marquee in the farm grounds. The farm foreman was Joe Millbank and the pig man was Bob Neave, who each lived in Wennington Hall Cottages along what became the A13 bypass. During the war an Auxiliary Fire Service unit was based at the farm, consisting of private cars with ladders carried on the roof and towed trailer pumps for firefighters. Prisoners of war used to help with the work on Wennington Hall farm and I remember one of them going missing. He was found next morning, asleep

Harry Gunary at the market.

next to one of the horses. Apparently the horse was sick and he wanted to stay by its side to make sure it was all right.

Alan Painter

The Land Girl

I was about seventeen or eighteen when I decided I wanted to join the Land Army. My dad wanted me to go into the WAAF as he'd been in the air force. In the end he gave in and my mother went with me to London to look for the recruitment office. We found the place eventually and after a lot of form filling, I had a strict medical and was accepted, then measured up. A couple of weeks later my uniform arrived in the post. I can't remember what we had to wear in detail but I know there was a hat, dungarees, jerseys, socks and Wellington boots, and a cow coat. A cow coat is a sort of cotton smock that we wore instead of an overcoat. I was excited as I tried the clothes on and felt wonderful in the uniform, but not the hat. I'd never wear the hat. The next thing I remember is my mum and I crying at the station when she came to see me off. I was billeted in a camp in Fen Lane, Orsett – it had been used by the forces and then for prisoners of war. One POW was still there and he looked after the fires. I liked living in the camp as there was always somebody to laugh and joke with and we girls had a lot of fun together. There was plenty of hot water for washing, and breakfast was always a cereal of some sort. We were given a packed lunch to take to work that always seemed to include a date sandwich! Our working times varied according to the light as we worked on the farms. I worked for Mr Vellacott at East Hall and had to get up very early in order to be on time to catch the lorry that ferried us to and fro. We had a supervisor who was answerable to the farmer and were given such jobs as vegetable picking – sprouts, spinach and the like, and in the winter did the hedging, clipping and ditching. I was only in the Land Army for a year before I met Peter, who was a Wennington lad and later became my husband.

Kathleen Gleeson

Kath Gleeson (right) – the Land Girl.

On the lorries

My husband worked for the Gunarys and drove the lorries for the farm. On Saturdays he and Mr Harry Whitby – who lived near Lenthorpe and was a farm worker – would go round the houses selling hundredweights of potatoes, then they'd both come here for some breakfast. They were great friends.

Vi Watts

Jack Townsend working on the Wennington nursery.

The field

In 1954 my father gave up his smallholding and bought the field in Wennington. At that time, the land alongside it was used as allotments for all the cottages. The allotments gradually disappeared and my dad took them over. The field at the back had cattle on it and the remains of the old concrete cattle trough is still there. The children from the cottages played round the back as well. When my dad bought the field he could have bought No. 1, New Cottages but he decided not to as it was war-damaged. He bought it later though, when he realised the damage wasn't too severe. He did a lot of tidying up on the field and began growing flowers and vegetables. He grew pinks, peonies, irises, wallflowers, sweet-williams, dahlias, gladioli and chrysanths. The chrysanths were both incurves and sprays. I'd help with bunching and we'd sell them at the gate on Friday nights for 2s 6d per bunch. We'd do that up until the frosts. During the day Dad worked at Rainham Sewerage Works but gave up when he got to sixty-five. That was when he made the little field into a garden centre and we'd sell plants and vegetables – we'd buy eggs and potatoes in. What my dad couldn't sell he planted, which is why the plot is so stuffed with plants and trees now.

Kay Knight

Chicken and eggs

I'd always wanted to do farm work and at one point the farmer took on a new manager who was interested in chickens. He offered me the job of looking after them. At the end of Church Lane there were two big rhubarb forcing sheds and they put a few thousand chickens in each one – they were bought as day-old chicks. They put another 500 chickens in what had been the old stables – I think they were Rhode Island Reds, the chickens that lay the brown eggs. We brought the chicks to point-of-lay and until they were strong enough they had to be kept in little tent-like structures and be checked every so often. The last check was at ten o'clock at night, so I took a torch with me and didn't think twice about going out in the dark on my own, even though we had no street lighting down there. That was in the late fifties and I did the job until about 1962.

I absolutely loved looking after those chickens. I used to collect the eggs and pack them into trays and they were collected once a week for sale. The farm manager taught me how to pick up a chicken and if one was injured I had a special tar preparation to paint on the wound – sometimes the chickens pecked each other. I had to feed them, of course, and on many a day I had to break the ice so they could drink. It was a seven days a week job. Fortunately I'd never worked regular hours so I didn't mind.

Elizabeth Wiegold

Cattle Lane

There used to be sheep and cows on the marshes when I was a child, and cows still graze over there. There was a farm over at Coldharbour where old Mr Vellacott used to farm. I'm not sure if there were farm staff

Farm horse and cart at Wennington in the early 1900s.

living over there but you could see little gangs of workers going over to Coldharbour from the Vellacott farm at East Hall. They'd go down by Cattle Lane by the brook, where the level crossing is, and we kids used to hang on the back of the hay wagons. I used to help the old shepherd in the lambing season. Besides East Hall, Mr Vellacott farmed at The Willows, and Ayletts at White Post Corner. He had his own blacksmith, whose premises were near the laundry.

Peter Gleeson

Home-made chutney

I revisited Rainham when my aunt and uncle moved into a bungalow in Cemetery Road, which I believe has since been renamed. It was off Upminster Road North and was little more than a made-up country road at that time. My uncle formed a partnership with his next-door neighbour and by combining their extensive gardens they created a jointly owned smallholding. They grew tomatoes and such in greenhouses and on the plot grew soft fruits, radishes, lettuces, carrots, potatoes... There were roses at the front of the houses. I remember raw beetroots being cooked in a cauldron. Any uncultivated land was used to keep chickens. My aunt sold the eggs from a table outside the bungalow as well as jars of home-made chutney and various jams. The two men bought a van and at weekends travelled to Canvey Island selling home-grown produce to residents, supplementing their stock with oranges and bananas for those weekend trips. The smallholding faced south and the view was marred by the huge rubbish tips that were the result of years of dumping London's waste onto the marshes. On windy

Wennington Hall
farm.

days the dust from the tips settled on the washing hanging out to dry. Then there were the flies and bluebottles which bred in the rubbish and plagued us all.

Robert R. Brown

The farmer's granddaughter

My mother was Gladys, one of the three daughters of Harry Gunary, the farmer, and she lived at Wennington Hall farm until she married my father in 1933. My mother went to get her bike fixed and met my father. He asked her out on a date. Her parents didn't approve of mother mixing with working-class people – she'd been privately educated and brought up to be a lady; but she married my father in Wennington church, and then moved to Aveley. Her sisters married well, but my father was brought up in a garage down the road, called Painter's garage. We'd visit the farm until I was about ten or eleven. Mum would take me to see the piglets and I can still remember the smell of pig meal in the barn where it was kept. They always had dogs but at one time they kept a bulldog in a huge kennel at the back of the house, just at the side of the door. It was meant to be a guard dog and they were all terrified of it, excepting the youngest daughter and the dog used to allow her into the kennel to feed it. My grandfather had a motorbike and as he drove off one day, the bulldog broke away from its chains and went after my granddad, and ripped his pants. The dog was ferocious and apparently couldn't stand the sound of the motorbike. Granddad had the dog put down after that.

Grandfather would go to the London markets every day on his horse called Dobbin and my grandmother reckoned he used to finish his sleep on the journey, as the horse knew his way. My mother told of a time when she and her sister, Muriel, decided to make a hole through a haystack so they could climb right the way through. It wasn't until years later they realised that had the haystack collapsed, they could have suffocated. She said there were lots of flies on the farm in summer and grandfather used to pay the children a penny for every hundred flies they killed. Goodness knows what he did with them. If my mother and sisters went out, they would be met at Rainham station by the horse and cart. My mother was allowed to work as a school teacher in Wennington school – she was eighteen when she started and was called Miss Gladys. My granddad looked ferocious sitting in his chair smoking a pipe, and when you walked into his lounge you could see all the cups he'd won for his farming. He was very Victorian and I was apprehensive of him, so I'd say a quick hello then the maid would take me into the kitchen and give me ice cream. The kitchen was big and had a scullery leading off it. I was a bit of a harum-scarum so wasn't very popular with my grandparents. My grandmother wasn't fond of children and although she employed staff to do the house-work, she'd do it herself, and leave the maids to look after them. Later they were sent to boarding school. My mother wasn't allowed to knit as my grandfather couldn't stand the clicking of needles. They grew asparagus on the farm and after she was married my mother was recalled to the farm to help pick it. I remember she'd balance a big bagful on her bike and bring it home, but we got fed up with eating it.

The old farmhouse had a lot of rooms and three cellars. I remember the smell of the fruit that was stored down there. Whenever I think of my grandmother I can smell bananas – goodness knows where they came from. There was a croquet lawn at the side of the house, and a summerhouse. When we visited we'd eat our sandwiches in the summerhouse. My grandparents never visited us, and I can't remember eating a meal at their house, but we used to receive a birthday card with 'love Grandmother' written on it. Beside the croquet lawn was a walled orchard where we picked apples – I think my brothers were sent for at apple-picking time and they'd come home with bags full of them. There were three white cottages belonging to the farm that still had gas lights – they faced on to the A13 – they were bought for the people that worked on the farm and I used to play with their children sometimes. There was a glass cabinet in the farmhouse they called The Admiral because my grandfather bought it when he won some money on a horse called The Admiral. They kept china in it and it was passed down to my mother. One of my brothers has it now as we didn't have enough room for it in our house, but I have a lovely picture of Venice that somebody gave my grandfather to pay off a debt. I remember they had a horrible ornament of an elephant with little squinty eyes. I didn't like it at all

but one of my brothers did, so it's with him in Bournemouth now. I think my grandparents were disappointed because they didn't have any sons to carry on the business and none of the grandsons were interested in farming, so eventually the farms were sold.

Frances Painter

Prisoners of war

Dad worked on one of the Wennington farms and during the First World War, he'd collect prisoners of war by horse and cart and take them to work on the farm.

Margaret Muscalla

Friesian cows

Mr Curtis from Berwick Ponds farm used to talk on the radio about his prize herd of Friesian cows.

Peter Gleeson

Arthur Blowers with farm workers on Coldharbour farm.

The farmer's secretary

When I became a qualified secretary in 1931, I went to see Mr James Spear Vellacott of East Hall farm to ask him for a character reference and since his secretary was leaving he offered me her job, which I accepted. I worked for him for about nine years. My work on the farm was most interesting – Mr Vellacott, who was in his seventies, was still very much involved in the farm and he was a Justice of the Peace. He was also Chairman of the South East Essex farmers' Union and a member of the Essex County Farmers' Union. Spear was a family name – there was a sleeping partner named Mr Spear who lived in Devonshire and there were quite a lot of Spears in the Tavistock area of Devon. They traded under the name of Spear & Vellacott. I worked from an office in East Hall and my hours were from nine o'clock until five on weekdays and every Saturday morning from nine, until I finished paying the staff their wages. I'd cycle from home to the farm. The Vellacotts farmed at East Hall, The Willows and Ayletts. An artillery battalion was stationed at Ayletts during the war. It was interesting, varied work and they left me to get on with it – they didn't keep interfering. I had to check all the market reports and work out the average price for every vegetable. I also had to check the timesheets and work out the wages for the lorry drivers. Mr Vellacott Snr was in charge of the work for the chapel in Cowper Road, so I dealt with all the correspondence relating to that. He was quite grand and I always addressed him as 'Sir'. There was a definite class distinction and the sons were addressed by their Christian names – Mr Millner and Mr Howard. Another task of mine was to make out the bills for vegetables that had been sold in Covent Garden market. I'd take the bills to the lorry drivers for them to hand to the salesman who'd deliver them to the customers. One of our most prestigious customers was Harrods.

Some of the men brought back the empty crates from the market and nobody was allowed to come home with an empty lorry. Those with no crates had to shovel up the dung from the yards then take it to the fire station in Barking to get it weighed. They'd get 6d for a ton of manure and when they got back to the farm, would have to shovel it off again to fertilise the farms. A lorry could carry four or five tons and the one that got back to base earliest, would go round to the three farms to collect produce to take to market the next day. Mr Vellacott didn't like anybody standing around doing nothing.

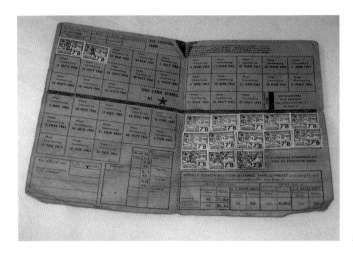

A National Insurance card, 1963.

Although they were supposed to finish at 5.00 p.m., in summer the farm workers stayed on until 6.30 p.m. or 7.00 p.m. – their basic wage was £2 10s per week but this could vary with overtime although they rarely earned over £4 per week. When I was looking after the books in 1931, it was compulsory for all those who worked to pay for National Insurance. Most of the folk around here were agricultural workers and the men paid 9d and the women 6d a week. That entitled them to get on to a doctor's panel. We only had one doctor in Rainham at that time and his premises were in the Wennington Road. Mr James Spear Vellacott owned a block of seven cottages in Cowper Road named Okehampton Terrace, and every Monday afternoon, I'd call to collect the rents. They varied a little but averaged about 7s 10d in the 1930s. A Mr Cleaver audited the books once a year and it took him nearly a week. Each September everything was valued – Kemsley's valued most things on the farm, and a Mr Roland Partridge from Chelmsford came up to value the horses. Mr Mallinson valued the cows and there must have been 300–400 of them as they were one of the leading farming families hereabouts, although the elder Mr Vellacott was more interested in cattle than in market gardening. It wasn't unusual for me to arrive at work to find he'd gone to a cattle sale for the day, perhaps Kent or Oxfordshire where he might buy 200 breeding lambs. They grazed on the marshes. The Vellacotts had two stands at Covent Garden Market and they also sent to Borough and Spitalfields Markets. Huge amounts of potatoes were grown. Seed potatoes were bought down from Scotland to be brought on under heat on Ayletts farm. They were one of the largest potato growers in the area but also grew cabbage, peas, beans, carrots, parsnips, asparagus, and the younger Mr Vellacott was interested in sea-kale. They grew daffodils too at East Hall, several varieties. Also the lettuce seeds were sown in cold frames between East Hall Lane and Church Lane. The Vellacotts farmed at Coldharbour too, but I'm not sure if they owned the land, or rented it from the War Office, because I can remember sending cheques to the War Office every year. Another little job I did was to take his wages to Arthur Blowers, the manager from Coldharbour farm, when he moved to Wennington Road. The blacksmith lived in New Cottages in Wennington during my time at the farm. Mr Brown was a very clever man – he'd had his own business in Brentwood that I think had possibly collapsed, and he came over to work on the farm. He could turn his hand to anything, not only did he shoe the horses but used to do all sorts of engineering work. He used to earn 1s 7d per hour and I'd stay in the office until he collected his wages on a Saturday. There were some cottages along the lane that led to Lenthorpe House and the blacksmith's shop was next to Lenthorpe bungalow where one of the lorry drivers, Jim Keeling, lived. Jim's father was foreman at Willows farm which was also owned by the Vellacotts. The elder Vellacott son lived in Lenthorpe for a time when he was first married and three of his children were born there, but I think the last one was born when he moved to Coombe House in Brentwood.

Ruth Daws

Pig sale

Twice a year, Harry Gunary at Wennington Hall farm used to have a pig sale – they used to come from all over the place to buy his Essex Saddleback pigs. He'd put a big marquee up on the side of the field. My aunt used to come from Wimbledon to buy Harry Gunary's pigs – I think she used to come for the hospitality as much as anything – she used to enjoy a glass of stout.

Peter Gleeson

Coldharbour, early 1900s.

Croquet on the lawn

My great aunt used to go over to the farmhouse in East Hall Lane where they had a ladies' afternoon on a Wednesday, and the lawn was so immaculate they used to play croquet on it. The farm shop in Wennington Road was a stable when the Gunarys lived in South Hall farm. They had two huge brown shire horses that were looked after by Mr Fitch – he'd take them to work in the fields. Those horses' backs were so wide he couldn't sit astride them properly, so he used to have to lean back with his legs projected out in front, as they clomped along the road. He wore this old brown coat and his legs were wrapped in sacking. When you turned right onto the A13 from East Hall Lane, you could see pigs in the field on the right-hand side. I remember the tin sheds. The farmer kept the pigs on one half of the field and grew asparagus on the other half.

Kay Knight

Coldharbour

I was told Mrs and Mrs Blowers from Coldharbour farm came to the Three Crowns regularly but I don't remember seeing any children, although I understand there were some. I don't remember going to the farmhouse but I do recall going to the stables and the barn. Their water supply was from a well and there was no gas or electricity either. The pub had a tank that held 10 gallons of water that we collected from Field's, the nearby factory. All the houses near the farm were the same, with no sewerage facilities either. They couldn't have a septic tank because a vehicle couldn't get down to the farm track.

Charlie Bifield

five

War Years

The post office

My parents were still in the post office in Broadway when the Second World War broke out. I helped out there during the war because it was extremely busy with lots of telephone calls and telegrams. We had to deal with the army camp at Ayletts farm and there were no end of Irish people working for Murex. They'd come in Friday evenings to send their money home by telegraph. We needed two girls on the counter, as well as Dad. All the letters were sorted at Rainham in those days and since Dad was in charge of the men, he was on duty at 5.30 every morning. There weren't many telephone lines in Rainham then but I was able to phone the telegrams direct through to Murex, which saved time. Others had to be delivered by hand. I remember on one occasion we had a telegram for someone who was serving on a ship that was anchored off Ferry Point and I can remember Dad ringing Mr Bifield, the proprietor of the Three Crowns, to check the ship was there. Somebody had to stand on the bank shouting for all they were worth, in order to get the crew's attention so the telegram could be collected.

Ruth Daws

Dances in The Hut

My brother was taken prisoner by the Japanese in the Second World War, so my mother decided to raise some money for the POWs by running little dances in The Hut. She and a chap called Monty hired a three-piece band, there was a piano, drums, and I think a guitar. We sold lemonade, cakes and biscuits, and Mr Grainger from the Lennard Arms supplied us with a barrel of beer. Since we didn't have a licence to sell beer, we charged for it in the price of the ticket but found out later it was still illegal. The dances were very well attended as there was little to do by way of entertainment. The girls came up from Rainham because all the men were away at the war, and the Home Guard used to come as well. I used to French chalk the floor during the day to make it slippery enough for dancing.

Stanley Byford

Bomb in Cowper Road

A bomb fell in Cowper Road and all our windows came in. We got to the point where we thanked God for every bomb that fell on the marshes because it meant one less for London. During the war there were wardens on the top of the telephone exchange opposite, and we said our house had a blue light outside because we gave the wardens cups of tea.

Grace Dalton

The dugout at Wennington Hall

During the Second World War, Mr Gunary had a lovely dugout built in the grounds of Wennington Hall farm, with beds and every-thing in it. When my husband and I were bombed out he invited us to use his shelter, along with Mum and Dad, which was very kind of him.

Vi Watts

AA Gun

To the best of my knowledge, no artillery ranges ever existed in Rainham. All sorts of handguns were used by the members of Rainham Gun Club, of which I was a member. The sand, used to absorb the impact of the bullets, was at one time sieved by hand by the army, and sold to Murex as scrap metal. I understand the Home Guard manned sand-bagged posts on the marshes adjacent to the factory during the war and the odd AA gun was displayed occasionally.

Ed Kimber

Wennington, 1940. Edna and Howdy Byford with Mrs Watson, Mrs Argent, Mrs Fitch and one other.

Cycling home

It was about half past four one Saturday afternoon, during the war, and I was riding my bike along Ferry Lane, just by Salamon's, when these German bombers came over. I looked up to see the sky full of them so I pedalled home like the clappers. The planes were heading for the London Docks but they dropped a bomb at Purfleet and the fire was alight all night. They had four big electric guns at Hornchurch Aerodrome but I don't think they ever shot anything down. They'd aim to keep the bombers high in the sky.

Stanley Byford

Observation

At the outbreak of the war, my Dad served in the Royal Observer Corps and I joined him at the age of sixteen. The Rainham observation station was on the roof of the old telephone exchange in Wennington Road – it's since been developed into flats, and is called Christina Court. Our call-sign was Peter 2, with Southend Pier being Peter 1, and Orsett, Peter 3. The post was manned for twenty-four hours a day and we did four-hour shifts, with two of us being on duty at a time. There was nothing between us and the enemy but our tin helmets, although I don't recall being afraid. In fact I was more nervous of climbing the stepladder that was laid vertically against the wall, to enable us to climb out to the roof. The area was very dimly lit and alongside the ladder was a tangle of telephones wires. Once on the roof, we plotted all aircraft coming over the South of England. Later, we'd see flying bombs come over and when the weather was clear, we could see the exhausts of rockets as they were launched from Holland.

We had to plot these too. We used a special plotting machine as all this was before the air force had radar. I became a member of the Air Cadets when I was fourteen and since I'd always loved geography, joining the Royal Air Force to do my National Service gave me the chance to go abroad.

Ted Davis

Anderson shelter

I was nine years old when the Second World War broke out and my father bought some huge pitch-pine beams that came from the big house on the Whybridge estate. He put them as a barrier in front of our Anderson air-raid shelter.

Dennis Payne

The airmen

My father told me that bonfires were lit on the marshes during the war to act as decoys,

so when the German bombers came over they thought they were above London. During this period, there was a compulsory scheme for Rainham residents who had enough room to billet airmen, and we had to take some. We usually had two but there was a time when we had three. They'd go out to the marshes to light the fires. Although there was a war on they really used to liven the place up with their jokes and music; one of their favourite songs was 'Star Dust'. Mum kept a cane on the table, and warned us she'd use it if we didn't mind our table manners. She wouldn't dream of really using it, but it kept us in check. It was always there, and even when the airmen joined us for meals, the cane was alongside her plate. They'd tease her about it and when the meal was finished she'd sit by the fire with the cane at her side and threaten them with it – jokingly of course. But one day she caught one quite a whack on the hand.

Margaret Muscalla

Big guns

Dad was in the forces during the war and Mum worked at Brigg's making jerry cans... All us children had jobs to do and worked hard, but we refused to go down into the shelters, despite the bombing. Then one night a rocket from one of the big guns in Parsloe's Park fell on the roof and we ran for our lives to the shelter. We went down there regularly after that.

Peter Smith

Messerschmitt crash

My dad had an allotment behind our house in Ingrebourne Road and a Messerschmitt came down there. I heard some years later that the pilot landed in the River Thames. There was a searchlight on Rainham marshes. For war work, my dad and my brother, before he was

Dennis Payne, 2005.

called up, joined the Home Guard and were based in the old police station at Chandler's Corner, so I used to do a bit of typing for them. We youngsters were never afraid because at that age you know no fear. One day, I was on my way home from work at Murex at lunch time, when there was a raid. I was watching a dog-fight that was going on in the sky and came off my bike. I was knocked out and when I came round, I was surrounded by soldiers who were billeted nearby. They rang my boss at Murex who sent his chauffeur to take me home and later that evening one of the soldiers bought my bike home.

Edna Harris (*née* Hawes)

V2 rocket

Just before the last war, we were living in Gainsborough Road when we began getting letters from the Government, telling us our house was in a dangerous area so advised us to find alternative accommodation, and move. This was because we were near Hornchurch Aerodrome. We moved to Oxfordshire for a while but were back home again by the time I was about eleven. I was combing my hair one Sunday morning when a V2 rocket fell and I was knocked out by the mirror falling on my face. I still have the scars where my face was cut about, but oddly, the mirror [frame] hadn't broken. A piece of glass hit Dad on the nose and my sister was cut on the side of her face. My mother had been at the kitchen sink and was taken halfway down the hall by the blast, and the back door had somehow preceded her and was lying further towards the front door.

Harry Sampson

Canadian Army

The Canadian Army were stationed on Frog Island during the Second World War, although I don't know why. As kids, as long as they gave us tins of fruit, we didn't care. There was a big army camp on Ayletts farm at White Post Corner, and there were thousands of Americans camped down Ferry Lane.

Peter Smith

Near miss

During the Second World War a plane crashed nearby. We were having a party in the back garden in West Close – we children were having fun, dressed up in crêpe paper dresses and hats. We looked up to see a plane overhead, and the pilot was waving at us, so we waved back. The engine was making a funny noise and the plane suddenly turned and crashed. It landed on the allotments at the back of East Close and we realised afterwards the pilot was probably waving us out of the way. The crew was killed but nobody else was hurt.

Muriel Sampson (*née* Ricketts)

ARP

During the war, on Sunday mornings, the ARP would go for training in the big house at Wennington. They'd go into the cellar for fire drill. There were no windows in the cellar just two big doors and in the middle of the room was a smouldering chair. It represented an incendiary bomb that we were supposed to put out. Boiler suits were worn, as was a white tin helmet. Nothing fitted, and if you were short, you'd trip over the legs of your boiler suit and the hats had no straps. You'd have to crawl along the floor with your hat falling over your eyes and the legs of your trousers getting caught up, while trying to handle a stirrup pump and a bucket of water. Unfortunately, by the time you got to the chair there was no water left in your bucket.

Stanley Byford

Tea party at West Close just before the plane crashed.

Wennington Detachment of the Home Guard during the Second World War, with Peter Gleeson at the far right of the front row.

Murex

There's no doubt that numerous efforts were made to bomb Murex during the war, but failed. This is borne out by the recovery of a complete set of floor plans, in which even the toilets were detailed. One assumes their main target was the new site on the banks of the Ingrebourne river, since that was where Murex manufactured the bodies of vast numbers of incendiary bombs. The latter would have been completed by another company, who added the starters and fins... At one time a member of staff disturbed a group of people on the path dividing the works and the Thames. They disbanded in a hurry, leaving behind the timing mechanism, wiring and items connected to bomb making – but no bomb! The insurgent culprits were never exposed.

Ed Kimber

Home Guard

When Wennington House was left empty, during the war, it was used to billet the Royal Artillery and when they moved on, it was used as a base by the local Home Guard and the ARP. The Home Guard did their training in there – George Grainger from the Lennard Arms was in charge of our branch.

Peter Gleeson

Welding bombs

I worked for Thames Board Mills when I got married but in 1942 I was transferred to Ford's. For the first few weeks I was gas-welding jerry cans as they went round on a belt. After a few months I was asked to become skilled at electric welding, which I learned at the Ford training school. I stood in a cubicle on my own, welding the tops on to bombs for five-and-a-half days a week. There were often air raids as I walked along Stanley Road North to go home. Shrapnel would be

whizzing all around me – but I thought of it as normal in those days.

Grace Jones

The Royal Scots

My older brother was in the in the Royal Scots but he died during the war and his name is on the memorial on the clock tower. He was a first-class mechanic so why they put him in the Royal Scots I'll never know. His name is also in the memorial book in Edinburgh Castle. When D-Day was set in motion we had an influx of troops in Rainham – they put them up in tents on the marshes. At one time the village was closed and we weren't allowed out – I think it was probably to do with D-Day, which was in 1944. We didn't really celebrate VE Day because lots of our lads were still in the Far East.

Edna Harris (*née* Hawes)

Rubble

My father became a crane driver and worked on the 'shoot' during World War Two. He said all the rubble from the bomb-sites in London was brought to Rainham marshes, and disposed of on the rubbish tip.

Margaret Muscalla

Tyre Week

We did collections to raise money for all sorts of causes during the war but I particularly remember Tyre Week – we all walked to school pushing tyres along – lorry tyres, bicycle tyres, pram tyres … all sorts.

Dennis Payne

Enamel dish

During the Second World War my husband was working on the Vellacott's farms so was

Margaret Muscalla on the site of the old Coldharbour Farm, 2004.

exempt from going into the forces. He had to take the produce by lorry through the suburbs into London and was really in more danger than some of those who were away fighting. He was in the Home Guard and I had to run all over the place to find him an enamel dish for his food, and a mug – I still have the dish upstairs – and his tin helmet.

Vi Watts

Stirrup pump

We always kept a spade and a stirrup pump close to hand, and one night we had an incendiary bomb in our back room upstairs. We dashed up the stairs and picked up the bomb on the spade and threw it out of the window. The field at the back was alive with incendiaries where a cluster had been dropped. There were no explosive devices in incendiaries those days, but there were later.

Stanley Byford

Zeppelins

I was born in 1907 and when I was a child I stayed with my grandparents at Freyerning, near Ingatestone. Grannie had a little shop there that sold everything. One night a Zeppelin crashed, near Billericay, I think. My uncle Wilf called out for us to put the lights out as it was suddenly so bright, but it was the lights on the Zeppelin. I remember it was all lit up as it came down. I saw the 101 when it came over Rainham too – I think it crashed in France.

Vi Watts

Clothing coupons

During the war clothes were on coupons but my mother managed to get hold of a nice piece of green Harris tweed to make me a jacket and skirt. There wasn't quite enough material so she bought some plain green cloth to go with it. She found a dressmaker to make it up, with the jacket in the tweed, and a gored skirt in the tweed with panels of plain green. I was thrilled with it. I used to go with my friends to Romford to get stockings, and new on the market were socks that came up to the knees, so I bought some green ones to match my costume. When I wore my new outfit the neighbours asked my mother what I belonged to. They thought I was wearing a uniform, so I didn't put it on again.

Edna Harris (*née* Hawes)

Nissen Huts

There were Nissen huts during the war, at the top of Sandy Lane in Aveley. Troops were stationed there, but after D-Day, were used to house prisoners of war.

Peter Smith

Eastwood Avenue

We had a dugout in our garden during the Second World War but were invited to use the double one in Penerley Road. The planes used to drop their bombs on the marsh on their way home – there must be thousands of them there still. There were lots of troops billeted on the marsh. There were five bungalows in a row just down the road from us and one day I looked up to see a doodlebug coming right for me. I tried to shut the door but the force was so great I couldn't. My face was paralysed for days and people said they didn't recognise me. The doodlebug hit a pylon and then fell on a bungalow, killing one chap and another lost an arm. All the bungalows in Eastwood Avenue were so badly damaged they had to be demolished, and they were all newly built

Demolished bungalows, Eastwood Avenue, 1944.

too. It was very frightening at times. That time, I lost my front door and my poor little canary was killed in the blast. His cage was smashed in.

Vi Watts

Edmund Road

On one particular Saturday afternoon during the war about 500 German aeroplanes were overhead and dropped a stick of bombs on Edmund Road. Only one hit a house, taking the side wall down, but the lady inside wasn't hurt.

Dennis Payne

Workers' playtime

A year before the war began we had what they called a crisis so they drafted a lot of soldiers into Rainham. They were stationed at Gunary's farm. I was about fourteen and forbidden to go up there. When the war started I took a job as wages clerk at Murex. People working for the company were exempt from call-up as Murex were working on something to do with the war. We used to have *Workers' Playtime* on and an admiral came to see us to give a talk about the war. We had to make our own amusement in those days so would go to dances in the Murex canteen, and to see films at the Princess in Dagenham. If there was a raid it came up on the screen and the film stopped, so you could either shelter there or go home. All the buses stopped running during raids so we used to walk home. It was a long way but we saw no fear in those days.

Edna Harris (*née* Hawes)

six

Shops and Businesses

Cutmore's

My mother was a widow when she married Mr George Cutmore who ran the grocer's shop in Laundry Cottages. We had a placard outside the shop advertising films that were on at the Princess at Dagenham, which was the nearest cinema. We sold a lot of bacon, cooked meats and cheese. The bacon came as a whole side, which, I think, was delivered every week. I can remember my mum having to take the bones out before it could be cut on a slicer, the cutter of which was turned by hand. We also sold luncheon meat, a kind of Spam and corned beef, which was delivered from the suppliers in large cans. Ham came as a whole joint, which again had to be cut on demand. The reps for the suppliers used to call once a week or fortnightly, to take the orders and groceries were delivered to customers by George Cutmore on a Friday evening. We

didn't have a phone until after the shop was closed in about 1963.

Paul Mudge

Candy's

I went to school in Rainham until I was fourteen. I left school on the Friday and started work on the Saturday in Candy's, a sweetshop in Whitebarn Lane, just off Broad Street in Dagenham. I worked there for forty-four years and eventually my husband and I bought the shop. There were terrible smogs in those days and sweets were in short supply in 1944. I only earned 17s 6d when I began work at Candy's and the bus fare was 2d so I used to cycle all the way. It worried the life out of my mother as we were still getting air raids. One day I heard the engine of a doodlebug cut out and some dustmen made me hide

Paul Mudge with his mother outside Cutmore's shop, 1952.

with them in an alleyway until we heard the explosion and knew it had fallen. We had few sweets in the shop (apart from pear drops), as they were rationed and I remember Dib-Dabs where you dipped a little lollipop into a bag of sherbet. There were Fizzies you could make lemonade from and if you sucked the lemon ones, your tongue would be yellow for about three days. We sold cigarettes, and Woodbines were 7½d for five, as were Players. Players Navy Cut were 1s 2d for ten, and we sold some horrible cigarettes called Stirling.

Muriel Sampson (*née* Ricketts)

Robbed!

When I was a child, Mr Hazell had the post office in Wennington and he used to peer between these jars of sweets – but one day he was robbed – he went into his cellar and he was hit over the head, so the shop was closed for a few days.

Frances Painter

The post office

When I was born in Rainham my parents, Mr and Mrs Holmes, had the post office in The Broadway. Dad was a stationer and sold everything under the sun – notebooks, writing-paper, envelopes, paste, crêpe paper, and inks of all colours – anything you could ever want in the stationery line. Mother sold drapery; all women's and children's clothes and haberdashery. She sold men's long-john pants, and also long grey socks for men that we called army socks – they cost a shilling a pair. There was wool, buttons, needles and cotton, but Mum also ran the post office. She worked for the Post Office before she came to Rainham – Dad was a postman, so that's how he and mother met. My sister and I had the most wonderful parents and Dad and I were great pals. In those days there weren't

any laws about the serving-age in shops so I was often allowed to help, while Mum and Dad would be in the back. As a child I delivered some of the telegrams when my parents thought it was safe to do so, and the Post Office paid 6d per mile. I'd get 1½d if it was near the shop, 3d for half a mile and 6d if I had to walk a mile. I wasn't allowed to spend the money I'd earned but had to put it into Savings Certificates, which cost 16s during the war. You put sixpenny stamps on a card until you had enough to get a certificate. People would come round selling the stamps during the Second World War. We sold sweets but as children we weren't allowed to take them just as we liked. We had to ask but I can never remember being refused. A bar of chocolate cost 2d. If Mum and Dad went out and we weren't going with them Dad would suggest we take a chocolate, so we helped ourselves to what we wanted. Dad left the retriever dog to guard us and of course it was safer in those days. We wore vests and woollen combinations because we only had one fire in the house, and there was just one tap with running cold water, and an outside toilet. I can remember seeing rolls of corsets in Mum's shop window, some were light grey and some were dark grey – they cost 1s 11¾d. Mother put ¾d on almost everything she sold. The men used to pass the post office at about 6.30 in the morning on their way to work with their dinner done up in a red hand-kerchief. The horse-drawn wagons would go by at about 8.30 at night on their way to Stratford market.

Ruth Daws

Saveloys and pease-pudding

There were no supermarkets as such when I was a child and I think the nearest thing to a mini-market was Green's at Rainham. The butcher in Rainham village used to open part of his shop on a Saturday night, and when the pubs and the social club turned out he'd sell things like saveloys, pease-pudding and pigs' trotters. The fish and chip shop also opened on a Saturday night.

Paul Mudge

The jeweller

I moved from Barking to Rainham when I bought a little house in Cowper Road in the mid-1980s. I was doing various jobs at that time, was out of work sometimes, but always wanted to go into business on my own. I'd had a friend whose father owned a jewellery shop, so I suppose that's the reason it always seemed an attractive proposition to me. I'm entirely self-taught but like to think I've become an astute businessman. I was still living in Cowper Road and unemployed at the time, when Margaret Thatcher's government brought out a scheme for the unemployed to start their own business. They offered to pay £40 a week so I jumped at the chance to go on a one-day training course. I can still remember a couple of things they told us. Seize the opportunity when it arises and don't be too cheap or you'll go under; but don't be too dear, or you'll still go under, even though you'll probably last a bit longer. You have to find a happy medium. Applicants could come out of the scheme at any time if it didn't work for them. I borrowed £1,500 from Barclays bank to buy a safe and other bits and pieces and went to see the owners of this block of shops. Number 8, Upminster Road South, which is on the end, was on the market for rent. They agreed to rent the shop to me for £50 a week but wanted a deposit as a goodwill gesture. I didn't have a lump sum to offer them and the shop was empty anyway so they waived the goodwill money and upped the rent to £60.

Rainham Goldmine.

That took the weekly allowance and more, so I had to make the business work. People warned me against opening a jewellery business in Rainham, saying it would never take off. The shop was so small you could stand in the middle and touch the walls either side, but I didn't care. It was mine, and at last I could go into business. I called my shop Rainham Goldmine and contrary to people's misgivings the shop took off, to the extent that people would queue to get in. The little shop took as much money as the bigger one I'm in now. By buying the right products and giving the right service, people came to trust me. My customers have seen my business grow and are very loyal. They travel quite long distances to deal with somebody they can trust. To me, the customer is always right, my prices are competitive and none of my gold is hollow, it's all solid stuff. It's easy to lose a fortune by buying the wrong product. I always like to have my affairs in good order so at the outset I found myself an accountant. I keep strict records and know exactly where I stand financially, and with my stock. Things were going along nicely when the block caught fire in 1991 and I was so relieved when the fire engines arrived, just preventing the fire from getting to my place, so I was able to carry on the business. I'd been renting the downstairs and upstairs of No. 8, while the remainder of the upstairs of the block had been used as offices. The roof of the building caught fire and the shops below were damaged, so I was the only one left in the terrace. The damage was such that the other shopkeepers had to move, and the owners wanted to get rid of the property, so beyond my wildest dreams, I was able to buy it. To do this I sold my Cowper Road house quickly and lived upstairs in No. 8 – there was no toilet, no shower, no bathroom. It was my office really and I used to lock myself in at night and nobody knew I was there. The block is Grade II listed, so I had to get everything restored properly and as the work progressed, it was regularly inspected by the council. It's the only listed terrace of shops in Rainham. The roof, main framework and most of the beams were repaired under the insurance policy and gradually I was able to get the restoration work under way and moved into the upstairs in about 1996. Two years later I was able to move the business to its present location at No. 4, Upminster Road South.

Jeffrey Tucker

Newsagent, tobacconist and confectioner

I wasn't allowed to read the newspapers in my Aunty Annie's shop, when I visited in 1929, but permitted to read the comics, providing they were returned to the shelves in as good a condition as I found them. I was occasionally given a small bag of sweets although the sweet

Jeffrey Tucker, 2005.

Frock Shoppe

OPENING NOV 7th

COME ALONG ENJOY A GLASS OF WINE
AND BROWSE THROUGH THE RANGE OF

* **DRESSES**
* **SKIRTS**
* **BLOUSES**
* **SUITS**
* **JUMPERS**
* **LEISURE WEAR**

**2 Upminster Road South
Rainham Essex**
(Next door to Butcher)

The Frock Shoppe opens.

counter, with its loose toffees and boiled sweets in jars, was out of bounds. I'd shoot at make-believe targets in the backyard with a toy bow and arrow, and play on a penny whistle.

Robert R. Brown

The Frock Shoppe

It was my mother's idea in the first place. She'd seen an advert for a clothes shop that was closing down in Rainham and decided she'd like to reopen it, so asked me to help her. I agreed, although somewhat reluctantly. We knew nothing about running a ladies' clothes shop, so before we signed the lease we went to a few wholesalers in Commercial Road. We looked around to see what was on offer, discussed prices and what quantities we had to buy... Some had a minimum purchase of 100 but in others you could buy single items. Mum went to an accountant who showed her how to keep the books, deal with the weekly takings, VAT and tax etc., and I still have the very first flyer from when we opened. We had to decide on a name and when we looked around the village nobody referred to a shop by its proper name, it was always the shoe shop, the greengrocer's, the baker's, the wood shop ... and because there was one of every shop, it seemed natural to name ours

Frock Shoppe. We spelt 'shop' in the old-fashioned way because our tiny premises were part of a listed block, so it seemed appropriate. Our address was No. 2, Upminster Road South. Our presence was announced with flyers in all the other Rainham shops and we opened on 7 November 1989. We began by selling blouses, skirts, dresses, jumpers and leisure suits which needed belts, so later we decided to stock accessories too. We started with costume jewellery and added anything customers asked for, really. Although we tried to stock underwear, the shop was too small to hold a big enough range. After about six months we were asked for children's clothes and some time after that, items of school uniform. It was only a part-time job for me at first as I kept on my regular job. I worked for Mars, taking the orders for confectionery from various supermarkets in the area. I did the buying for

the business with my mother, besides working for two or three afternoons in the shop. Disaster struck when about two years later our premises caught fire. I was at home on the Sunday, a week before Christmas 1991, when somebody rang to say the burglar alarm was going off in the shop, so I thought I'd better see what was happening. When I arrived, I was surprised when I saw the number of fire engines. In the event the whole block was on fire, and reported as the biggest fire Rainham had ever had, with fire engines coming from Rainham, East Ham, Barking and Dagenham, even as far as Kent. It seems the fire had started after work had been done in the roof, but the problem we were faced with was water damage. We still had a ceiling but everything above that was destroyed. With Christmas looming, the butcher next door was stocked to the brim with poultry. Apart from the water

Fire crews attending the listed block of shops.

we had a little smoke damage and some of the clothes were unharmed but we had no front door, as it had been kicked in by the firemen. We managed to retrieve some clothes and the police and fireman helped us form a chain across the road to the Holiday Shop and shoe shop, whose owners kindly stored them for us temporarily. Mum was at the wholesalers buying more goods while all this was going on, so when she got back to Rainham there was nowhere to put it. Still, at least we had some new stock. We were closed for about four months and opened again the following April. Meanwhile the owner of the bridal premises, My Fair Lady, allowed us to put two rails of clothes in her shop so we could trade for the week before Christmas. People had put deposits on clothes for Christmas so we needed to honour their orders. We began trading again in April but within three days had a burglary, because we had no proper roof. Burglars put a foot through the ceiling, so we were unable to get insured again. All through the summer we continued to conduct our business but acted like a market stall, taking the stock home at night and back to the shop in the morning. We did that for six days a week – it took us two hours in the morning to load the clothes into the car and the same in the evening – so we traded from 10.00 a.m. until 4.00 p.m. The lease on our shop expired about four years later which was about the same time as the owner of My Fair Lady closed down, so we took over her lease and moved our business to the opposite side of the road where we stayed until June 2004. We got to know the size and styles of our customers so well, we'd buy items from the warehouses with them in mind. 'That's a Pat blouse,' we'd say, or, 'Maureen would like that skirt' ... and we were always proved right. I must say I enjoyed my fifteen years trading in Rainham. Customers would come in to browse and have a chat, and I'd often make them a cup of tea. We had an old TV and some people came in especially to watch *Kilroy* or *Neighbours* – it was that sort of community.

Jenny Chaproniere

Jenny Chaprionere.

Old Fishy

There was an old chap in Rainham who rode round the streets selling fish from his bicycle trolley during the week and at weekends he sold ice cream from the same trolley. We called him Old Fishy because his ice cream smelt of fish. Fishy had a shop by the cemetery – it was little more than a shack, really. He sold Fro-joys which were an ice cream on a stick, and Sno-fruits. He'd ride around the village calling out 'Stop me and buy one', but didn't sell Walls' ice cream.

Muriel Sampson (*née* Ricketts)

Chandler's bakery

My uncle Albert and my Dad, Frank, took over the bakery in Rainham from their father, Albert Chandler Snr. The bakery was on the

Frank Chandler with family members. Note his rather large hands – he was a baker by trade.

old A13, and the site has now been officially named Chandler's Corner. They say the ovens still exist in the back garden but I've not been back there for years. I only vaguely remember my granddad working there when I was a child. There was a door in the roof of the main bake-house and this was where Miller's used to deliver the sacks of flour. When a bake was about to start my dad or his brother, (or sometimes his son, Albert Chandler Jnr) would climb the ladder that led up to the loft space and tip few big sacks of flour down the wooden chute into the mixing bowl beneath. In later years they bought a stainless-steel mixing bowl that was about 5ft in diameter. The right amount of salt was added, by the handful, then yeast that had previously been mixed with water. When the dough was ready, the bowl was tipped slightly and they'd cut into it, then gather a big piece into the white aprons they wore, and plonk it into a trough.

The trough was made of wood on the outside and metal on the inside. It was like a horse trough, really. They'd cover the dough with hessian sacks, then put wooden boards on top and leave it to prove and rise in the warm atmosphere. My dad used to take a nap on top of the trough and when the dough had risen sufficiently, he'd be tipped off, so knew it was ready when he landed on the floor! Then a big rough piece of dough would be cut out, and again this would be carried in their aprons to a bench. It would then be cut, weighed and put into the bread tins. They always seemed to get the right amount first time. The loaves went into tins and were cut across the top, pasted with water and sprinkled with seeds, depending on which loaf it was. There was one lady who liked the crust almost black, so one would be left in the oven longer, especially for her. There was a huge black oven in the bake-house. The roaring fire was fuelled by coke – it still puzzles me how they used to know when the oven was at the correct temperature for baking. They used long wooden 'staves' for putting the bread in the oven and to take it out when it was baked. The whole place was warm and had its own unique smell. Whenever I smell freshly baked bread I think of the old bakery. When he made buns my father used to get two bits of dough and lay them on the table then roll them into shape with the palms of his hands. This was done simultaneously, in a circular movement. He had enormous hands and it was fascinating to watch him because he did it so quickly. Everything was done by touch. They knew just when to get the bread out of the oven by touching it, and just how much mixture to put into the containers. Each loaf went into a tin and if one came out of the oven flat dad would say, 'It's run out!' It was still edible though. The bread was put on to metal trays and carried on one hand at shoulder height to the 'shop'. In later years, as he got older, this job was done by Albert Chandler Snr, just so he kept his hand in. I can't remember all the cakes

they made but I know there were shortbreads – my uncle seemed to make most of the cakes because he went on a course. The Atora van used to deliver suet direct to the bakery. My dad took a picture of the canvas-covered wagon that was pulled by two bullocks. It was going round the Rainham lanes at the time. The owner of the wagon, Mr Hugon, used to travel all round the country selling unrefined suet to his customers. They'd refine and use it in their baking but I've no idea what dad and his brother used it for. Often the Ford workers would pop into the bake-house on their way to work in the early hours of the morning, to get freshly cooked rolls. There was no baking done on Sunday but in the afternoon, they used to go in and start the fires again, ready for the overnight baking for Monday. Dad sometimes let me go on his rounds with him. The van mainly had bread in it but there were shelves around the inside where they carried a few odd tins of corned beef, baked beans and such, just in case somebody had run out. When the van went round the corner all the tins would fall down and I used to love tidying

The Atora wagon making deliveries.

The Three Crowns pub, as depicted by a mural on the river wall at Rainham.

them up for him. I'd stack them neatly into rows, but I'd get in the way, and Dad would tell me off.

Ann Waller (*née* Chandler)

Local shops

Mum had no need to go to the shops very often when we were children, as nearly all the shops delivered. Arthey – the baker, came round the door, as did the milkman and Dexter – the butcher. Even the Maypole delivered all through the war. The Maypole kept our ration books and brought our weekly entitlement plus anything else Mum wanted. She'd give her order on a Monday and they'd deliver on a Friday.

Dennis Payne

Life in the pub

My dad kept the Three Crowns pub down at the end of Ferry Lane. We went to live there in 1923 when I was six years old and the only son in a family of girls. I had seven sisters. The only help I was allowed to give was to collect used glasses in a basket on a Sunday. Three of my sisters were married so my brothers-in-law used to come down to help, and Mum and Dad used to serve. Mum and my sisters did all the catering at the pub – weekends were very busy. Everything was coal-fired, Mum used to make up ten to twelve midday meals and they were all cooked on a little kitchen range. The plates were heaped up with meat and veg – that must have been in the twenties and early thirties – meals used to cost 1s. There was a big garden at the back of the pub where dad used to grow the vegetables for the pub meals. We also sold Rainham Ferry rock – in two sizes, the smaller costing 1d and the large one 3d. The laundry was done in a coal-fired copper and when teas were wanted – mostly on Sundays – Mum used to boil the water in the copper that she'd used the previous Monday to boil the washing in. But we all lived to tell the tale. In fact Dad lived to be ninety-six and mum and my sisters, into their eighties. There were millions of flies down there – I've never seen anything like it since. Even when I was in the services overseas I never saw flies like there were in the pub. We had fly-papers in every room but in no time at all they were full up. Mum also had these wire cage things with a little tray at the bottom that she used to pour beer into. The flies were attracted by the beer and would come up inside the cage, so there'd be hundreds of them in the kitchen that would end up in the cage. Anyway, they'd still be alive so mum would put them in the oven and cook them. Within twenty-four hours she'd be cooking the ten weekend dinners for the customers in the same oven – but we all lived. Being near the river, there were mice and rats in the pub, of course, so we had three cats to keep them down. We also had three dogs and my favourite was called Crownie but he turned out to be a sheep chaser. Flocks were kept on the marshes and when it came to sheep dipping, Crownie was off chasing them. There were always police around at that time, and I'm afraid Crownie's life ended. We knew the shepherd, Jock Newton – he had a bit of a shack on the marsh and supplied milk straight from the cow. Ferry Lane was just that, the road that led from the village to the ferry. The people who came at the weekend used to come on the buses and trains, not by boat. The average wage at that time, if anybody had any work, was about £2 per week, so people were very poor. They used to come down to

us for an outing on a summer Sunday, literally hundreds of them. I think the takings on one day were £3 6s, and bearing in mind that beer was only about five old pennies per pint (2½p nowadays), I suppose it wasn't a bad day's takings. It was mostly weekend trade, practically nobody came in during the week. There were only eight cottages near the pub, I can't remember what the occupants all did for a living but one was a waterman, working on the river, one worked for Whites, the barge repairers and builders, one had a shop in his front room, some worked at Murex, and one other chap lived in a hole and he did no work. We called him Tamey. Then there was the Winn family who lived on the Murex site because the father worked there. There were the Whitby and Ross families too. All we children would walk to school together. There was no ferry boat at Rainham when we lived there but I understand there was in previous years. The only seafaring people we saw worked on the ships that used to tie up at the buoys. There were floating anchor places by the ferry, and dad said he made most money in 1926 during the General Strike, when there were a dozen or more ships out there. The crew would be paid off and the first place they saw in this country was the Three Crowns, and that's where they spent their money. Dad used to joke, saying, it was the money he made during the strike that enabled him to put the deposit down on the new house when we moved out in 1936, but I don't know if that's true.

Charlie Bifield

The forge

I grew up on a farm near Colchester and wanted to follow my father into the farming business but he said, 'no way', so I eventually served my time to become a blacksmith. I worked at several steel fabrication places

Above: David Wright at the forge.

Right: Wennington signpost, designed and crafted by David Wright.

before deciding to start my own business trading under the name of Thameside Forge. My son works with me and we moved the business to Wennington, from the city farm in Barking about seven years ago. We were originally a few buildings along from our present location but there was a serious fire about three years ago and the old place was destroyed. This site is ideal because there's plenty of room for storage. There's a staircase going into the roof where we keep the iron. There's talk of my moving into Rainham village but because of the noise the forge makes, I doubt it will come off. I sometimes have to work into the night and that wouldn't be very nice for the people who live nearby. I made the Wennington signpost after submitting a design that was accepted. Everybody seemed to be pleased with it. I enjoy working on my own designs and that particular job brought me to the notice of the council, so I began to do work for them on jobs such as restoring the weather vane on St Laurence church in Upminster. I'm working on some parts for the Upminster Windmill at present. Besides working on some other notable projects, I did a lot of work at Arundel Castle and on some gates in the Port du Clichy area of Paris. Although I work on more important assignments, I still do everyday things, right down to sharpening shears, knives and even lawnmowers.

David Wright

seven

Entertainers and Entertainment

The boxer

I was the youngest of four boys and my father was a docker. Mum died when I was about six years old and Dad brought us up on his own, so we missed out when it came to home life really. I earned pocket money by doing odd jobs and funded my school trip to Trewern myself. Trewern is a residential outdoor centre in Ross-on-Wye where we kids could do such things as caving, camping, canoeing and pony-trekking. It's part of my nature to want to be the best I can, so when I took up boxing as a youth, I made sure I was successful. I boxed at featherweight and won many competitions. I was captain of the Barking Amateur Boxing Club and also represented England. I was an NABC finalist, London ABA champion and PLA winner of 1978-79. My cups are all stored away now but there must be over 100 of them. I have fond memories of the teachers at my school, who made sure I had extra sports lessons because they wanted me to win. I was the youngest ever winner of the London Federation of Boys' Clubs title and the competition was held at the Café Royal in 1975. My teachers realised I'd need a boxing robe but I didn't have the money to buy one, so they clubbed together for the material and made a robe for me. It was in white with red trimmings – complete with hood. You can imagine how proud I was when I wore it and carried away the trophy, with my dad and all the teachers from Eastbury school watching. I boxed at several London hotels after that. I went on to qualify as a boxing coach and it was my ambition to be a sports teacher but I realised early on that I'm more of a doer, not somebody to sit down and study for exams.

Victorious Jeffrey Tucker, aged seventeen, after a toe-to-toe fight at the Mill House.

Howdy Byford at the speedway track.

I was always better at sums than English, and gave up coaching in 1990 when I went into the jewellery business.

Jeffrey Tucker

The speedway rider

My brother, Howdy, went to work for a plumber who at some time was given work at West Ham Stadium. Since we'd always been interested in bikes, it sparked off Howdy's interest in speedway racing. Howdy and I built a little speedway track on our garden – the gardens in Church Lane were on the land opposite – so we had quite a bit of room. When he first took up racing I used to act as his mechanic, but gave it up when my wife and I had our first child. There was a special smell at the speedway and it was due to the oil they put in the tanks – it was called Castrol R. Howdy was a bit of a character and used to sing at the track with Eric Chitty – they even made a record.

Stanley Byford

West Ham Stadium

As teenagers, one of our favourite pastimes was speedway racing at West Ham Stadium. We'd catch the train to Plaistow then the bus down to the track. Our favourites were such stars as Aub Lawson, Malcolm Craven, Eric Chitty and Howdy Byford. The stadium held 1,000 people and we were addicted to the

smell of the oil and roar of the engines as the riders sped round the track. We'd all be in a frenzy of excitement, but never caused any trouble.

George Barrett

God bless his memory

Howdy Byford was our second cousin and he lived with his family in the coffee shop at Wennington. During the war he was called up to the Essex Regiment, so, prior to his going, we went to Wennington to wish him farewell, and he walked us back home. As we came down the alley and into the house, Mum and Dad were having their nightly prayer-time and they were praying for Howdy's welfare and safe return. He went to Singapore with his regiment and was taken prisoner of war. People used to say, 'If Howdy comes home', but I always said, 'When Howdy comes home',

because I knew our prayers would be answered. Later, while working in the post office, I had the tremendous thrill of taking off a telegram from San Francisco. It was addressed to his mother and said, 'I'm alive and well'. Howdy returned to a wonderful career as a speedway rider but sadly, he died several years ago.

Grace Dalton

The circus performer

Mum and Dad met in 1906 when they were working on the stage. My father's stage name was Ihonart, which is a contraction of Iron-Heart, because he was so strong. He was a weightlifter, boxer and wrestler and kept up his strength by eating huge steaks. Mum was an acrobatic dancer and when she and Dad married in 1912, they went to live in Ilford and Dad opened a gymnasium where he taught weightlifting... They had seven children

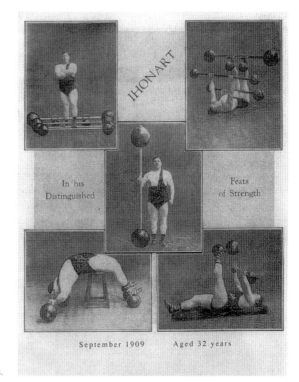

Opposite: Howdy poses by Stan Byford's Jowett.

Right: Ihonart, the weightlifter, father of Grace Jones.

and we were trained to be acrobats from the age of three as it's necessary to start while the bones are still flexible. Since we were always training we had little contact with the outside world and other children. My first stage appearance was at the Ilford Hippodrome at the age of five. I wore a little red two-piece with a red garter and was to perform a solo act of acrobatic dancing. I was so nervous when I saw the sea of faces that was the audience, I burst into tears. Mum called me off the stage and my sisters and brothers took my place and did their act. Meantime, my mother took me to one side and explained that the audience were nice people who wanted me to do well, and had paid to see me, so I must do my bit. I returned to perform and when I finished my act the audience applauded and threw money onto the stage. That year, Dad decided to join Bertram Mills' Circus. Strict regulations are applied to travelling people so my parents

needed to belong to the Showmen's Guild. We did no travelling from Christmas to April and during this time Mr Mills went around the country booking up different sites. Our first venue with Bertram Mills' Circus was on Nanny Goat Common at Becontree Heath. I remember the goats on the open ground. Mr Mills paid rent to the council and in turn, the performers paid him footage, which meant the bigger the tent the more you paid. Dad paid footage because the tent where he did his weightlifting was outside the Big Top, but the rest of the family weren't charged because we were part of the main show. Children weren't allowed to be given the money they earned, it had to be saved into a trust fund until they were twenty-one, but I think we were given a few pounds each week for expenses. We lived on site in a caravan. One of Mr Mills' functions, when he was looking at possible sites, was to ascertain where the toilets and water were, also the nearest public baths. In those days practically every park had toilets and running water, so we'd use what was there. The nearest baths when we were at Becontree were in Barking, where, for sixpence, they'd give us a towel and a bar of soap and we'd have a lovely hot bath. Travelling with us were an ice cream man, a confetti man, candy-floss man, and an American man selling sarsaparilla. These men were there to pull the crowds in. The confetti man would sell it by the bag to the boys who'd chase the girls and throw it over them – the girls would run away screaming – it was all good, clean fun. When we were on the move, we were unable to travel during the day because many small towns had tram-lines that were difficult for the horses and caravan wheels to negotiate. We had to go slowly and didn't want to cause traffic jams, so travelled at night when there was little traffic on the roads. There were no brakes on the caravans and carts, so when we reached a cattle trough the vehicles had to be scotched by bricks. We'd watch the steam coming off the horses and throw a blanket over them in case they caught pneumonia. When they were fed and rested, we'd continue our journey. We were taught to ride bare-back and stand upright on the horses' backs as they trotted round the ring, and also to balance on the tight rope. Circus life was wonderful and all the performers were one happy family. We travelled until 1930 when it became illegal for children to work on the stage because their education was neglected – up to that time we'd had no schooling. We were performing near Church Elm Lane in Dagenham at the time the new law was about to come in, and one night there was a violent storm. All the tents were blown about and the equipment badly damaged so Dad decided it was time to leave the circus. My parent's belongings were stored in a massive trunk and during the storm, it was stolen. Because of this we have no early family photos, except copies of those that appeared in the press or for publicity purposes. The trunk was so heavy it took two men to lift it – it contained everything we owned and we were left penniless. When Mum and Dad were travelling they invested their money in a big entertainment company and the children's money couldn't be touched so although we were comfortably off, there was no ready cash.

Grace Jones

Grace Jones, 2005.

eight
Local Events

Bonfire night

There were lots of parties when we lived in Nelson Road. There always seemed to be a party in somebody's house – there was real community feeling. In those days we'd address the neighbours as aunty and uncle. Mum collected all year round for the bonfire night party which was as big an event for us as Christmas. We had a big open garden where we'd have a huge display of fireworks and take along our guys to be thrown on to the fire. We'd cook potatoes and chestnuts and one year, when the fireworks were stacked against the French doors, a spark must have got to them. The explosion was quite frightening and I remember running down the garden in panic when a rocket whizzed past my ear. The dog wasn't keen on fireworks after that.

Derek Chaproniere

Coronation of King George VI, 12 May 1937

In 1936 I had a Jowett car, then bought a new Ford for £145. I dressed it up with ribbons for the Coronation in 1937 and we all lined up on the village green.

Stanley Byford

Carnival Queen

My dad entered me for the Carnival Queen competition in 1990 and as I was only fifteen years old and very shy, I didn't tell my friends about it. Dad took me along to the competition dance at Britton's school – thank goodness he did because I didn't know anybody and was very nervous. There were other girls there and during the evening we were taken aside by three judges and asked such questions as, what age we were, what we did for a living, what our hobbies were... I was still at school so it was a bit nerve-wracking. Later we had to walk around so our deportment could be judged. They also wanted to see how we'd react to meeting people because, should we be chosen we'd have to attend charity events. They called the name of the girl chosen to be the princess first, and after that the girl to be queen. I was quite shocked when my name was

Stan Byford and his mother with his new Ford car, decorated for the Coronation celebrations in 1937.

called and I realised I was to be the Carnival Queen. The local press were there, and my parents who were really proud of me. I was given a maroon sash with the words 'Carnival Queen' in gold lettering and a maroon cloak. They're still in my mother's loft.

We went to Romford to buy the dresses from the couple who ran the Torchlight carnival. I was Carnival Queen for three years running and we had pink dresses for my first year and white for the evening. In future years, we wore white for both day and evening functions. I think our dresses were donated by the wedding shop, My Fair Lady, for the second year. We were able to choose the style of dress we wanted and they were cleaned several times during the season as the hems got very dirty. The selection dance was held at Britton's school again for my second year, and at St George's Hospital for the third year. The carnival was always held on the second Saturday in June and the season went on until September, so we were taking part in processions every Saturday, followed by a dance in the evening. There were rarely any boys at the evening functions we attended but when there were, they had to request permission to dance with us from our chaperones, who were Don and Ivy Poole. It was all quite formal and my dad was pleased about that. During the dances there would usually be a competition for Queen of Queens, or Court of Courts – the court being the queen and her princesses. Again, this could be quite intimidating as we'd have to show how well we could curtsey and be questioned again, but it's surprising how we got used to it. The Carnival Queen from the previous year always acted as the current queen's deputy and since we were thrown together for so long, the queen, deputy and princess always became friends and I still see some of them fifteen years later. We received a gift on the first day of the carnival – usually a necklace which we wore throughout our reign and we also received a gift at the end of the

Carnival Queen Sharon Logie (*née* Harvey) and deputy Wendy Nunn, 1991.

season as well. I'd feel quite excited wearing my lovely gown while sitting on the flower-decorated float. On the day of the carnival the taxi that pulled the float would be waiting for us at the library, then we'd go on to Britton's farm where we'd join the rest of the floats and other carnival courts for the commencement of the Rainham carnival procession. It was a long day and we were always very hungry at the end of it, so rather disappointed when we were given a salad for dinner. The procession ended at Spring farm Park where there were stalls and various entertainments, so we'd stay for a while then go home to get ready for the evening when we'd welcome the courts from other areas. During my reign I met local dignitaries and I felt my confidence grow as the season went on. I was Rainham's Carnival Queen for three years and look back on those times with great pleasure.

Sharon Logie (*née* Harvey)

Gospel outings

The little Gospel Hall in Cowper Road was run by old Mr Vellacott, the farmer. He was a lovely man and at Christmas time or New Year you'd get a prize, the value depending on your attendance. You got your little text every week as well. In summertime Mr Vellacott used to hire a train and take us all to Southend for the day, and pay for us to have tea in a restaurant. He really was a dear old man. I think the name of the restaurant was Garon's. Mr Vellacott did so much for the community – and all the girls used to meet up on Wednesdays. There were boys who I think came from an East End Mission and a character we knew as the Captain used to bring them to Rainham and they'd entertain us. Mr Vellacott used to allow them to pitch their tents and have a bonfire on his farmland, and they'd have a singsong. Also, he had tennis courts that we were allowed to use.

Edna Harris (*née* Hawes)

Havering half-marathon and fun run

I was involved with the Havering half-marathon and the fun run, which began in 1984, for about eighteen years. Since I was Head of Year at the Chafford school then, I felt I should take part and volunteered to help put all the records on computer, and eventually looked after the admin. The Chafford school with South Havering Rotary Club instituted the events with Unigate (later Dairy Crest) as the main sponsors. Many parents, led by Derek Godden, took part in the organisation of the event. The third Sunday in May was a great day out for local people. Parents organised the car parking on the school playing field and the event was combined with such things as a bring-and-buy sale, various stalls and displays, and a craft fair in the school hall. It varied from time to time and one year the local kite club gave a kite-flying display and another year

we had helicopter flights. Sue Ospreay and her Lightnin' Drama Group arranged many of the displays and she was also very good at organising the stalls. I suppose there were about 250-300 runners in the half-marathon and 900 in the fun run. The fun run was open to anyone and many children ran with their parents, grandparents etc. Some parents even ran with toddlers in buggies. I think they ran a distance of about five kilometres. Their route was from Chafford school through the village, up to the Cherry Tree pub, through Cherry Tree Lane, along the A13 and back down to the school. I think the biggest response we had was 600 for the half-marathon and 1,200 in the fun run. The half-marathon people went right out through the lanes to Upminster, along Harwood Hall Lane, up through Little Gaynes Lane, looping round into Gaynes Park Road, along Corbets Tey Road to the traffic lights, then on to Roneo Corner and back to the Chafford. It was a full half-marathon and the distance of thirteen miles was

Havering half-marathon and fun run medals.

Stewarding the Havering half-marathon and fun run.

carefully measured and planned. Quite a few local notables ran, including Paul Freedman. Paul, like nearly all the runners, got himself sponsored to raise money for charities. When Tilda Rice took over the sponsorship, they usually sponsored an international runner and they brought them and teams of employees and families along to take part. There was a cross-section of runners – some people came from the Channel Islands for three or four years, some came from Ireland, and at least one chap came quite regularly from Holland. We had quite a few elderly people and some professional runners. The event was advertised in the running magazines and people who were in the country on holiday took part – we even had some people from Australia one year. One chap came down from Durham to race in his wheelchair, in fact several people raced in wheelchairs. The first runners in the half-marathon would be back in just over an hour because the route wasn't hilly, and several of them were pretty keen club runners. What we called watering stations were sited along the route with people handing out cups of water and sponges. Derek Godden was very good at rounding up volunteers, as we also needed about 120 marshals along the route to ensure the safety of the runners. We made donations to their chosen charities in appreciation of their help. Over the years charities benefited from the distribution of many thousands of pounds raised by the runs. The winners of each race were given a trophy and everybody who passed the finishing line received a medal. There were different medals for the fun run and half-marathon. It was a very popular event and Trevor Brooking, the West Ham soccer player, came regularly, as did many prominent local people and the MPs of the time.

Jon Polden

Maid of honour

I remember the carnival very well and in the 1930s one of my friends, Gwyneth Long, was one of the maids of honour.

Edna Harris (*née* Hawes)

Toffee apples

On bonfire nights we'd have a lovely time on the village green in Wennington. There was a driver who used to bring a load of wood on his lorry for the bonfire and somebody else did the roast potatoes. My wife used to make the bread puddings and somebody else made toffee apples.

Peter Smith

Gigs

We had a youth club at the end of the road but I wasn't a member. I was learning to play the drums at that time so was in Dagenham a lot, with my group. I remember a gig at Triptons College and another group who played there called The Rapiers. Our group was named The Chequers, possibly because my pals lived near the Chequers pub. My brother played the guitar and we started working together in such places as the Rainham Working Men's Club, La Salette school and the Silver Hall Social Club. I still play now. In my twenties we used to play in the Whybridge Community Centre and over the years have done several gigs there, and even performed at a street party in Nelson Road.

Derek Chaproniere

Carnival association

Rainham had a carnival before the Second World War but of course it had to stop when the war began. Then in 1973 Havering Council organised a Festival of Havering, and a few local people decided it might be a good idea to do something in Rainham. We formed a little committee and planned a small carnival as part of the Festival. A Miss Rainham was selected and we held a street procession which raised £98. People enjoyed it so much it was decided to resurrect the annual carnival, so we formed a Carnival Association and included the whole of the Rainham postal area. I helped get the scheme going and eventually took over as chairman of the committee in 1982. The carnival and street procession went on for thirty years and took a lot of organising. A dance would be held somewhere in Rainham, most of them at Chafford's, where we'd select and crown a Carnival Queen and two princesses. The girls would have two dresses

Norman Wright (RAPS member) at the carnival, 1939.

Carnival, 1939. Vera Keeble as Carnival Queen, with Gwyneth Long (right) and Joan Valentine (left) attending.

for the year of their reign – they'd have a float dress and one to wear for evening events; we bought them from several places. There was a wedding dress shop in Rainham some years ago, so we got some from there, we also bought them from Debenhams, and elsewhere. Sometimes the dresses would be given for nothing and sometimes we were able to obtain them for a nominal fee. The tiaras were replaced nearly every year but some lasted for two years with many of them being donated by our president at that time, Mr Jack Broad. The queen and her princesses had busy summers, taking part in other carnivals in the surrounding areas and in winter attending dances to support the functions of other carnival associations. I think our highest street collection was about £900. We had to apply to Scotland Yard for licence to do a collection, and all the money raised had to be donated. We supported several charities – some that come to mind are a

commode chair for the hospital, dartboards and installing equipment for the handicapped, and a donation of £1,500 towards the building of the ROYALS, the youth centre near Tesco. The only money we took out was the cost of the insurance. The various carnival associations would support each other by sending floats … and an average Rainham procession would involve about twenty-four floats. We began the organising each January and the carnival took place in June. Our float would take part in carnivals in the surrounding areas when our own carnival was over – the season finished in about September. The procession started in Britton's playing fields making its way through to the Cherry Tree, stopping off at the Dovers Estate for about half an hour, where they'd supply us with refreshments. We'd then make our way through the village, and back across the A13 at Chandler's Corner down to Spring Farm Park. We pulled away at about 1.30 and it took about three hours for the procession to reach its destination. We'd run a float for a couple of years then change it. Everybody pooled their ideas and helped with the construction. At some point, we were given a taxi to tow the float with, and the chap who ran Rainham Taxis used to maintain it for us. It was out most weekends when we attended other people's carnivals and again at Christmas. We'd have great fun at Christmas, going round the streets with Father Christmas on a float lit up with fairy lights, and playing carols. We'd collect money for Christmas parcels to be given to the Rainham housebound elderly.

Don Poole

Village fête

Wennington used to have a village fête and we'd put all the decorations up with Union Jacks and the like. We'd play at throwing the Wellington boot and have coconut shies. We had some great fun in those days.

Peter Smith

Princess Margaret's wedding

We had a lovely street party for Princess Margaret's wedding and another when the road had its 25th anniversary.

Derek Chaproniere

Nelson Road party for Princess Margaret's wedding to Anthony Armstrong-Jones, 6 May 1960.

nine

Places of Interest

Whybridge Manor House

Whybridge Manor House was empty and backed onto our plot of land; the present estate is named after the old manor house. We loved to explore the house when we were children, our footsteps echoing as we ran in and out of the empty rooms. My brothers loved playing in the old kitchen that was in the basement, swinging on the iron hooks that would have been used for hanging meat. The house had a caretaker who had a wooden leg and if he found us he'd chase us away and naturally we loved provoking him. We discovered a couple of priest-holes, one of which had a secret entrance with steps leading to the roof. As we made our way up the steps the caretaker found us and chased us on to the roof. There was no escape so we jumped off into a bed of stinging nettles about five feet high which wasn't a pleasant experience. I once saw a horse in the orchard – he was eating plums directly off a tree which was laden with fruit. There was a large barn in the grounds and at night, we could hear owls screeching, which could be quite frightening.

Mary Bell

The swimming pool

We members of the Residents' Association sat down one day and talked about what Rainham needed in the way of amenities, and decided we'd like a swimming pool. We persuaded the officers to do a report on the borough, to show which areas didn't have access to a swimming pool, and Rainham hadn't, so we made sure one was built. The pool is attached to Chafford school and is for school use during the day, and on evenings and weekends is open to the public.

Don Poole

Wennington House

Mr Green, the owner, spent a fortune on the gardens at Wennington House. He had a

Whybridge Manor, as seen from the smallholding.

mulberry tree and four or five walnut trees. There was a vegetable garden, and a sunken garden with a fountain that was operated from a well that he and the sons sank themselves. The gardens were set out in different sections. As you went into the grounds to the left, by the village hall, there was a fishpond with a waterfall and that section was filled with dahlias. Separating that was a hazelnut hedge with a bed of carnations on the other side of the bank. The beds were cut in four quarters of the moon with a star in the middle, all filled with different flowers. The grounds were on a slope so he made a sunken garden, with terraces made up from slag from the Murex works. As it was metal waste, it shone in all the colours of the rainbow. There were four little gardens round a fountain with different flowers in each one. I remember the forget-me-nots and pansies, all the plants they used were different. Then there was a lovely rose garden. Everything was laid out formally. The front of the grounds was laid to lawn with a crazy-paved avenue up to the front door and a bed of roses in the middle. A row of roses stood on either side, firstly a standard rose then a bush rose. There was a side door for the tradesmen, and a pair of big gates used for the cars to drive through. Ethel was the uniformed housekeeper and there was at least one maid. During our breaks, when we were helping Dad out, they'd bring us tea and slices of bread and butter for us to eat in the potting shed. The house was about three storeys high, with folding shutters over the windows. We were only allowed in the kitchen – it was huge with a big range and a laundry room at the far end. When Mr Green left, my father was appointed caretaker until the next tenant moved in, so we were able to wander all round the house then. A big boiler stood in the basement and there was also a wine cellar. One of the main rooms led on to a large conservatory where a huge eucalyptus tree was planted on one side – it grew right up to the roof. On the other side of the conservatory, on the outside, was a plumbago that went right up the wall – its flowers were pale blue. They used to grow gloxinias, begonias and the like in the conservatory – it was quite tropical as it was heated by the boiler. The whole house was centrally heated. Down the side of the house were three massive geraniums that were trained to grow against the wall and old George Brennan, who used to live in the cottages by the ferry, used to take cuttings from them each year in the little potting shed. They'd be grown in pots and planted out in the garden each spring. There was another greenhouse along the wall by the road where more plants were grown, and was home to two huge grapevines – it was one of my dad's jobs to thin them out. Mr Green used to pay us boys, my brother and I, to water the gardens – there were stand-pipes all around the grounds. Each year we'd help my dad plant thousands of bulbs – dad did the dibbing and we'd go behind him popping the bulbs into the holes. There were two sons in the Green family, Tony and Bunty, and we used to play with them as kids. Bunty took over the business when Mr Green retired, but he didn't live at the House, which was demolished some time later.

Peter Gleeson

Bowls Club beginnings

During the 1960s, one of our members was very keen on bowls and thought it would be a good idea for Rainham to have its own bowling club. We put a notice in the library asking for interested parties to get in touch and when we saw we'd get enough support, began the process of forming the club, which is still flourishing. The site chosen had been the Murex sports ground. The council had received a planning application for building

Bowls Club in action, 2005.

houses on the site but there was a public uproar at the threat of losing an open space which was zoned as a sports ground. So, we won the day and agreed to have houses built on half of the site with the other half remaining an open space. The bowling club was then built on part of the open space. The council told us they had an old prefabricated building that Cranham had turned down, so we took it to use as the clubhouse.

Don Poole

Rainham and District Rifle Club

I became interested in shooting after I got married. My husband joined the shooting club so, rather than be left at home, I decided to learn myself and came to love it. It's a very companionable thing – we'd come home after each session, have a cup of tea and clean our guns together, while talking about our day. After a while I took over as secretary, organis-ing the shooting venues etc. I've belonged to the club for forty-two years but only deal with the membership side of things now. The first meeting of the Rifle Club was held in the Phoenix Hotel in December 1946 and the club then went under the heading of 'D' Coy 14th Essex HGOCA RC, and consisted of ex-members of the Home Guard. In 1949 we were instructed by the authorities at that time, to rename our club, hence Rainham and District Rifle Club came into being – since both Rainham and Purfleet ranges were used. When we eventually produced our club badge it depicted the Essex emblem and the Thames connection. Membership expanded and in the late sixties reached over 300 personnel from all walks of life. You'd be able to enrol at seventeen but it wouldn't be much fun as you'd be quite isolated and it's necessary to be introduced by another member. Nowadays young people under the age of seventeen aren't allowed to handle a gun alone so have to be accompanied by an adult. They have a probationary period of about six months but it can be longer if we think it necessary. The probationary period applies to all members joining the club. People who join shooting clubs are devoted to their sport – it takes a lot of skill to hit a target. Some of the men are very proud of their guns and are always on the look-out for really old weapons. They inspect them and weigh with them in their hands, look at the quality, the mechanism etc. – they really love the technicalities of guns. At one time we provided facilities for pistol, rifle and clay-bird shooting within our club and when the Rainham site closed, we used the Purfleet range for about five years until that was disbanded as well, so we use several sites now, much further afield. Current legislation is very rigid and it's not possible to cater for all disciplines. We enjoyed our days on the ranges – we'd take a flask of tea and some sandwiches and spend the whole day in the fresh air. There used to be a large population of skylarks nesting on the marshes – and sheep grazed on the land when the shooting was in progress. Dogs were not allowed on the ranges at all.

Margaret Humphrey

Rainham Rifle Club emblem.

Kent View

People didn't have a lot of money just after the Second World War. Careers had been interrupted when the men were called up for war service etc. and, what with the bombing, private rental and council housing was very scarce. My husband's interest in self-build was sparked by a notice he saw in the local papers – those that were published in the Goodmayes-Seven Kings area. A meeting was to be held in the hope of finding enough people who'd be interested in building their own property. He went along and when he came home was very enthusiastic about the scheme. Initially there was a group of about forty people who were interested so the idea progressed. Obviously things didn't happen overnight but after several meetings a committee was formed and the Seven Kings Self-Build Association came into being. It was decided that everybody would like a semi-detached property and throughout the project, everything was decided on a majority vote. Details such as: 'did the downstairs have one large room or two smaller reception rooms', were put to vote and it was decided on the latter. Also the majority didn't want the stairs to be seen from the front door, so the staircase goes up the middle of the house. The first step was to find enough land to build forty houses, but finding enough space in the area of Seven Kings or Goodmayes proved difficult so they began looking eastwards out of London. However, while they were searching for land, the group knew they needed professional abilities and although they had electricians and carpenters, the rest of the men agreed to go to evening classes to learn a skill. My husband's choice was to learn plumbing and he went to evening school for two years. The committee felt they should go ahead with the plan for forty couples although they accepted some people would drop out. Eventually only twenty of the initial forty went ahead. We weren't able to choose our own fittings when the houses were built – everything was built to a standard – and in the fifties you were limited to what was available. They found the first plot of land in the Goodmayes area and we all contributed towards a deposit – I think our share was about £5 – and fifty years ago that was quite a lot to us, but the owner ran away with our money so that particular deal fell though. I'm not sure who discovered the land at Wennington, but we bought the site of the old Wennington House. I think it was quite run down, as prisoners of war were housed there during the Second World War and the land had been used for allotments. It was a dank November day when I first viewed the site. A 6ft wall ran all around the property and at first glance, it looked very dreary. However, it all looked entirely different when the wall was pulled down. Construction began on the ground either side of the building, leaving the demolition of the house until last. There were trees that had to come down... I think by the time the old house was sold off, the gardens, which I understand had been beautiful, had deteriorated. Building began and the first pair of houses were officially opened in the summer of '54. The scheme was funded by the Ilford Borough Council and each man had to complete a minimum of sixteen hours a week. Strict records were kept and the men could put in more hours if they wished. In the winter they worked under floodlights and in between using their skills they had to do the labouring jobs. At the end of the project all the hours were recorded and those that had put in the most had a smaller mortgage. As each house was occupied the owners paid rent to the council, but when the whole scheme was completed and wound up we were all given mortgages by the council. Since the council were involved, the buildings were inspected regularly and everything was done properly. The Byford café was open on Sundays when the men were working, but in fact, when the first two houses were occupied, the owners used to make cups of tea for the builders and I did the same, but people still used to go to the café. When we saw the first pair of houses completed we really knew what the development would look like. We had an official opening and the local mayoress came along, as well as the vicar and other officials from the council. They used one house for people to walk round to see what had been done, and the other to provide refreshments. One man dug over the two front gardens and having bought a bunch of fresh flowers, he stuck some in the ground and they looked lovely, giving a nice finishing touch. Of course, when we got the key to this house we were elated. We'd been living in a couple of rooms with my mother-in-law and couldn't believe the space we now had. My husband and I took possession of our house in January '55 and it would have been '58 when the last pair was finished. As each house was completed it was

Share certificate, Seven Kings Self-Build Housing Association Ltd.

ALL THEIR OWN WORK!

IN the house he helped to build himself, Mr. Edward Griffiths and his wife entertained the Mayoress of Ilford to a cup of tea on Saturday.

Six semi-detached houses in various stages of completion, were the centre of much excitement in the village of Wennington, Rainham, and there were extra police to control the crowd when the Mayoress stepped out of her car at the gates of 20, Kent-view, which is fully built.

She had come to open the first house built by the Seven Kings Self Build Housing Association.

This association has 23 members, all people who have lost all hope of being found homes by local authorities, and have taken the matter into their own hands by building their own houses.

They are planning to build 17 houses on the site at Wennington, and they should be completed in 8 months more.

They laid the first brick on the site on September 6 last year, and one house is already finished. The next two will be ready in September.

As the houses are completed they are allocated to members of the Association on a points basis.

When the Mayoress opened the front door of 20, Kent-view, she handed the key to Mr. Griffiths, and then with Ilford councillors and officials she inspected the house.

There were no carpets or linoleum, nor any furniture, for Mr. and Mrs. Griffiths and their two children won't be leaving their home at 12 Clandon-road, Seven Kings, to move in until this week-end.

SPACIOUS ROOMS

After the Mayoress had looked through the three bedrooms and four spacious downstairs rooms and admired the excellent paintwork and good craftsmanship she sat down for a well-earned cup of tea.

Later, Mr. Griffiths stood proudly at his front gate, watching the entourage disappear down the narrow, winding road, and casually said "Of course, I am a bit excited at having a house of our own at last, but I don't show it. My wife is more excited than me."

(Photo: Byers.)

THE MAYORESS (Mrs. C. A. Headley) at one of the houses built by the Seven Kings Self Build Association at Wennington on Saturday.

Right: The first house at Kent View is ready for occupation.

Below: Kent View, 2005.

allocated on a points system – just the same as the council operates – those with most need came first and after several years it was noticeable that the children at one end were older than those at the other – as couples without children were housed last. When the whole development was finished we had a party to celebrate. Almost fifty years later there are five original owners still remaining in Kent View.

Elizabeth Wiegold

Social hall

In 1958 the social hall was a Nissen hut near Parkway and the Residents' Association managed to get a new one built at Chandler's Corner, behind the police station.

Don Poole

La Salette

When we first came here we used to go to the small Catholic church opposite the mission hall in Cowper Road. Our church was just a hut really. It wasn't far to walk because there was no Dovers Estate then – the ground was part of Poupart's farm. We'd take the footpath between here and Cherry Tree Lane, then cross a ditch that had a couple of planks over it, and on to the farm. We'd climb over a stile into a small wood and cross the road into Cowper Road. I would have been six or seven then and was not allowed to miss church on Sunday. There were no main roads in those days so we were quite safe. Alfred Poupart died in 1937 and in 1938 the American Church of La Salette bought the land. La Salette converted a barn into a church in 1939 and we began to worship there. The presbytery where the priest lives was the farmhouse. There was a wonderful orchard where the big car park is now, and the parishioners would pick the apples and sell them at the corner where the gates are. A permanent church replaced the old one in 1967.

Mary Bell

The ROYALS

In 1990 I was approached by the home-beat officer, Charlie Merrion, about starting up a youth club in the village. I was born in Rainham and had a good childhood so I thought I'd like to give something back to the community. I attended the Sunday school run by the parish church, and went to the church youth club on Monday evenings. At that time the youth club was held in a little hut that's no longer there. Charlie introduced me to Sue Gooding who was working with the youth at that time, and after several meetings we decided to form a committee. We kept it small initially, as we wanted to begin by raising enough funds to get the project off the ground. We called on the services of Margaret Andrews who along with Dick and Ellen Beasley had run stalls for the carnival. They used to work very hard at baking cakes, and we knew they'd be good at getting some money in. We knew Dick and Ellen were experienced in working with young people, since they used to run the 813 Youth Club before it closed. The club had been based at Chafford school so they'd bring a wealth of experience to the scheme, apart from working hard to make some money to enable us to get started. We realised we'd need many thousands of pounds to provide a purpose-built youth centre. I'd been on the carnival committee for about fifteen years so was used to fundraising and had served as a councillor for short time, so knew council procedures. The first meeting was held in July 1990 with a committee of five or six members. We had to choose a name for the club and came up with ROYALS, which stands for Rainham Organisers for Youth Activity Leaders. Our aim was to get the club built, then leave the running of it to the youth leaders – we'd have no further involvement. We approached quite a few companies for sponsorship and some of them responded with money. Apart from doing house-to-house collections, we raised money in several other ways. We held football matches etc., and the National Trust gave us permission to hold a fête in the grounds of Rainham Hall which proved to be very successful. Gradually the money began to come in. In the latter part of 1992 Mary Ball was invited, and agreed, to join the committee. Mary was a councillor and had lots of connections and knew council policy, so we knew she'd do a good job for us. Negotiations with the council for a site began in 1994 and the London Borough of Havering put the piece of land near Tesco at our disposal for the youth club. In the same year we became a registered charity. As such, we were then able to approach the National Lottery Fund which meant filling in lots of complicated forms. An architect was appointed

and English Heritage became involved. Since Rainham is so rich in history there had to be a site dig before the area could be cleared, prior to the start of building work. At this point I had to resign from the project as my job in the City had become more pressurised, but I still managed to do some fundraising. The National Lottery provided a grant of £60,000 in December 1995.

Kathy Gibson

The Bowls Club continues

I was on holiday in Spain with my husband, Charlie, when we first became interested in playing bowls. We saw people on a green so decided to have a go ourselves and when we returned home, thought we'd get some practice in at the police club at Chigwell. Unfortunately it's quite a few miles from Rainham to Chigwell and each time we went there it always seemed to rain, so we took the plunge and applied to join the Rainham Bowls

R.O.Y.A.L.S. CENTRE
FOR ACTIVITIES AND EVENTS
PHONE 01708 525601

The ROYALS

Club. The rest, as they say, is history. Rainham Bowls Club was formed in 1976 and we play lawn green bowls outside in the summer season – which is from May to September. We play indoors from October until the end of April and the rules are the same for both formats. Singles games are played between two players and the first to score twenty-one points is the winner. Doubles are between two pairs and the pair with most points over twenty-one ends are the winners. Triples are teams of three players, the game being decided over eighteen ends. Rinks are made up of four players on each side, bowling only two woods each, over twenty-one ends. Although bowls is moving with the times by allowing us to wear coloured shirts and blouses etc. traditionally our dress code has always been grey trousers or skirts with white tops, in practice and club games. We continue to wear white trousers,

Maureen Merrion.

skirts and tops when we pay in a friendly and club competition finals, and the same for district, county and national competitions. Until recently, ladies were required to wear a regulation hat on the green, but now the wearing of hats has become optional. We organise friendly matches in such places as Eastbourne and Hastings and travel by coach on these occasions, and a match is played against the host club. The membership book is open and at present we have about 120 members, with the membership being split with 45 ladies and about 70 men. The club celebrated its Silver Jubilee in 2001 and as I was in my second year as captain of the ladies' team, I was called upon to help with organising the celebrations. Coincidentally we were able to lay a new lawn on the green that year too, as we'd been given a grant by the Cleanaway Trust. One of our ladies, Mrs Pat Brown, was President of the Essex County Women's Bowling Association in 2003. During that year she had to organise several county games and the Essex County finals at Rainham Bowls Club. Pat has also served the club for many years as the Ladies' Secretary. We don't have cooking facilities at the clubhouse so usually lay on a cold tea for friendly games at the weekend but when we had our Silver Jubilee celebrations and Pat's County Executive game, we managed to provide hot potatoes with the meal. The men made these meals special by waiting on us ladies and organising the car park. We're having a big extension built at the moment because the clubhouse wasn't very big – the ladies' changing rooms are being extended and last year we were given permission to have a bar, so we should be able to have a few social events, during both the open and closed seasons. We have a presentation evening in November and this is when trophies are presented to the winners.

Maureen Merrion

The library and the day centre

When my wife and I moved to Rainham in 1950, the only facility it had was a library that operated from a shop. In the late 1960s the bakery in Brights Avenue came on the market and we persuaded the council to buy it, so we could have a proper library. At the same time Stanton's Radio, just opposite the church, went bust and it was the council's decision to put the library in the vacated building. We were then left to decide what to do with the Brights Avenue site – and that became a day centre for the elderly.

Don Poole

Statues

I remember the big old house that stood in large grounds of what is now known the Whybridge Estate. A wood ran between Nelson Road and Stanley Road and there were also lakes. We'd fish in the lakes – there were several types of fish but my father reckoned he caught mainly tench. They say people used to skate on the ponds when they iced up in winter – but that would have been before my time. There were lots of statues in the gardens and extensive grounds, although I believe it was sold off in the 1930s and the house pulled down.

Dennis Payne

The organist

Although I play the organ in several local churches, my preferred instrument is the piano and I'd say my favourite composer is Grieg. I also accompany the choir of the Townswomen's Guild – they have about fifteen members and meet at Fairkytes in Hornchurch. They give a concert about twice a year in St Andrew's church.

Ted Davis

Ted Davis.

Horticultural Society trading hut, 2005.

Horticultural society

I'm chairman of Rainham Horticultural Society. I don't have time to do much gardening myself but I like to go to the hut occasionally to help out. I went on to the council in 1962 and it was in the Horticultural Society's constitution that they made a local councillor an Honorary Vice President and I've been with them ever since. The allotment holders on Parsonage farm were the founders of the Society, which meets at the Methodist church on the corner of Ellis Avenue once a month. They also have the trading hut in the Upminster Road South. They have their own greenhouses and the hut is open on Saturday and Sunday from about 10.00 to 12.30 to sell members' produce, flowers and fertilisers... They'll weigh the fertiliser up in small amounts so you don't have to buy a large bagful. It only costs £1 a year to belong to the Society and they have about 1,300 households on their books now. One year a member grew a prize parsnip in a dustbin with the bottom cut out. The roots of the parsnip grew through the dustbin and into the ground – it must have been about 3ft long. They have a general gardening group and a ladies' floral art group, and hold competitions in the church hall.

Don Poole

ten
Reflections

Green Line bus

I saw the advert for No. 13, New Cottages in the Wennington Road, in an Essex newspaper in 1954. I was working on the buses at the time and my husband was retiring, so since I was fed up with living in London, the idea of living somewhere peaceful appealed to me. I came to view the cottage on the Green Line bus and the fare cost me 1s 2d. I wasn't too sure I liked it when I looked over it because it looked old and run down, but we took it anyway and did it up. Later·we moved along the road to No. 7 because it had an extra room where my son could have his friends. We had an allotment that I think we paid £5 a year for.

Dot Barrack

Good timing

We could see right across to Rainham clock tower before the houses were built around here on the Whybridge Estate. One chap

Peter Smith.

reckoned he'd watch for the 103 bus to leave the clock tower before walking to the Cherry Tree in time to catch it.

Dennis Payne

New house

I was married with a couple of children when we first came to live in Wennington. We'd been living in a flat in Melville Road, Rainham for about five years and after the war, housing was short. The vicar talked to the council on our behalf and on 1 April my wife told me we had the pick of four houses which were newly built on Wennington Green. As it was April Fools Day I didn't believe her at first but we were over the moon when we were invited to pick up the keys. That was forty-nine years ago and I've loved every minute of life in Wennington.

Peter Smith

Rough shooting

As a boy, my father, along with his two brothers, his father and dogs, would go across to Erith on the ferry-boat and do a day's rough shooting over there. They were all ex-military so were fine marksmen who had their own shotguns and rifles. Some of the proceeds of this sport were eaten by the family and some of it went to the dogs – so everyone benefited. When they wanted to go home they'd signal a man on the north side of the river to come over and collect them.

Ed Kimber

Stars in the sky

One of my most vivid memories of life in the circus is travelling in an open truck at night, being lulled by its rocking and watching the night sky alight with stars.

Grace Jones

Salamon's vehicles.

Cutting the grass

Mr Oliver lived in the little thatched cottage in Church Lane before the Ayres took it over – he used to cut the grass in the church-yard and have a little pony and trap. There was a family named Challis in there, before Mr Oliver.

Peter Gleeson

Isolation

While my family lived in the Three Crowns pub there were only two local buses – they were run by Edwards and Stephens – and they catered for the factory workers. It wasn't a regular service and we wouldn't have used them to go to school. We always felt safe as children, walking the one-and-a-half miles to Rainham school. Nobody was unsafe in those days. Very few people used Ferry Lane except the Murex employees who'd be at work by the time we set off. They'd mostly walk to work although one or two had bicycles, but none had cars. The only vehicles we saw in Ferry Lane in those days were the two steam wagons belonging to Murex, and their staff car. Then there was the Salamon's tanker truck. Salamon's was a chemical plant that converted waste products from the gas works. Very few cars came down the lane at all.

Charlie Bifield

Visiting the river bank

I recall visiting the river bank with friends as a child. We walked along Ferry Lane sing-ing 'I'm Happy when I'm Hiking' and other popular songs we'd learned from the wireless. Sitting on the sea wall, we ate our cheese sandwiches, supremely content as we watched the murky river flow by.

Robert R. Brown

Houses at the end of Ferry Lane, c. 1920.

Open-topped bus

There were only three buses a day from where we lived (near the Cherry Tree) to Rainham village in the 1930s, so we'd walk there through the unmade roads. We went by open-topped bus to Romford and thought it great fun when the bus went under the railway arch in the Upper Rainham Road; the conductor would remind to us to duck.

Grace Jones

Cycling

There was little to do for entertainment when I was a teenager, so we used to walk a lot. I didn't go bluebelling myself but people would come from miles away to pick the bluebells round here. When I was older I was allowed to cycle to Wingletye Lane in Hornchurch to see my aunt and uncle. When I was bigger I had a bicycle so used to get around on that – there was a man near Blewitt's who had a wooden shed and did up bikes and mended them. My dad bought my first bike and later the young man I was courting won a beautiful bicycle in a raffle. It was a ladies' bike with dress guards and three speeds, and he gave it to me. That was in 1926. Sometimes I'd stay in Hornchurch overnight and my aunt, who had worked in service, taught me how to cook and do all manner of housework. Rainham did very well for shops in those days – there used to be three Green's stores at one time.

Vi Watts

Residents' Association

My father always used to say, 'there's no place in local government for politics' and when, in 1959, somebody knocked on the door canvassing for the Residents' Association, I joined. Then they asked if I'd be the road rep to distribute the magazines along the road and pick up any comments from the residents. After that they asked me to be an area rep, which entailed dropping off bundles of magazines to the road reps and picking up any feedback they'd collected. After some time I was given a place on the executive committee. I was rather shy in those days and it took me some time to adapt to my role but once I got used to it, I took a great interest in local affairs. I'm Chairman of the Residents' Association now and we meet once a month. I became a councillor in 1962, because of the unmade roads in the Parsonage farm area. Some allotment holders from the Prince Regent's Lane vicinity of the East End had bought plots of land from about £25 per plot. Between the two world wars it became normal to see men get off the train at Rainham carrying their gardening tools. Edwards and Stephens, a local bus company, ran a bus to ferry them from the station to their plots and sometimes the whole family came as well, staying overnight in the allotment huts. Eventually proper dwellings were built on the sites. Apart from unmade roads they had neither sewers nor street lighting and in 1958 they decided something should be done about it. They were told by the council it wasn't a priority, so the Residents' Association decided to sort it out. We had a live wire on the committee at that time. His name was Leslie Nichols and we put up him for election to the council. He got in and served for three years, so was able to get the Parsonage farm programme started and I and the other residents' councillors saw it through. Thereafter we were represented on the council for some twenty-three years. We had all the roads made up and were responsible for most of the facilities in Rainham.

Don Poole

Tom Brown

Tom Brown was an old rag and bone man who lived in Blewitt's Cottages at one time. He'd go round the streets collecting unwanted things and squatted in an empty house round here for a time, and died in there.

Dennis Payne

Pushing baby

I'd push the baby in the pram from Rainham to Wennington when I came up to see my friend, Charlie, and I'd walk past the Wennington House on my way. It was becoming neglected then, and later was pulled down.

Peter Smith

The bicycle ride

My aunt used to live in an old farmhouse that was let into two parts. There was no sewage and they used oil lamps. It was in New Road and had a huge garden with the toilet right at the bottom. When my cousin needed to use it, she'd get the bicycle that she kept outside the back door, and ride to the end of the garden.

Madeline Fatharly

Shooting

Our pub opened on a Sunday from 12 p.m. until 2.00 p.m. and again from 7.00 p.m. until 10.00 p.m.. Beer was so cheap people would get drunk in the morning, fall down and sleep it off in the afternoon, then get up and start drinking again in the evening. Just in front of the pub there were some posts where they used to moor barges, and often the men would put a penny on a post, stand in front of the pub door and fire their shotguns to see who could hit it. It should have been quite an easy shot but after about ten pints they'd miss. It was quite safe because they were firing out to the river. Most of the people living near us had shotguns and they used to shoot seagulls on the marsh. They'd spend their money on the ammunition but not on food, so they'd eat the seagulls, but we didn't.

Charlie Bifield

El Dorado

As a child, my favourite ice cream was manufactured by El Dorado. They did a flat ice cream in different flavours – I always had lime and it was delicious. It cost a penny but if you only had a ha'penny, they'd cut it in half.

Harry Sampson

Spending wisely

I was married in 1941 and went to live in Stanley Road North, then Hubert Road. We rented our bungalow at first and when we were given the chance to buy it, I paid for it outright with the money I earned in the circus.

Grace Jones

Captain Pinchbeck

My family have always been involved with the Gospel Hall. Mr James Spear Vellacott,

Charlie Bifield gazes wistfully over the site of the old Three Crowns, 2004.

who started it, was a wonderful man. He was a farmer and my parents first met each other while they were working for him in East Hall farm. Women's meetings were held on Wednesday afternoons and Mum used to take me with her when I was a baby. I've always loved children and have done Sunday school work, youth work, and girls' classes – all at the gospel hall. Once a year we'd shut the school and hire a whole train to go to Southend – we went to Lockhart's for tea. Mr Vellacott would always see to it that when we had tea somebody gave us a talk. We used to have little pink, blue or green ribbons and we'd walk from the Gospel Hall to the station. There was a Captain Pinchbeck who used to run a youth club in the East End somewhere, and he and his boys used to come down to sing to us and speak. At the end of Cowper Road was a dairy run by Charlie Flint and it had an awning out the front. After the gospel service one Sunday night the Captain and his team stood under the awning and gave a talk to whoever was passing by. Vellacott's cattle would have been on the marshes at Rainham and then there were the rifle ranges at Rainham and Purfleet. It those days Rainham was a village with a village community. There was a lady opposite who was not well and I remember Mum putting a kaolin poultice on her. The doctor at that time said it was the first time a neighbour had done the right thing.

Grace Dalton

No electricity

The pub had a septic tank and a horse-drawn wagon would come on occasions to empty it. We had a garden of about half an acre or so; in-between times, I'm afraid it was a case of just digging a hole and pouring the sewage in. The farm was some half a mile from the pub and there were three cottages beside the farmhouse. It's all grassed over now. We had no electricity or gas in the pub, so used oil lamps and a wood-burning stove for cooking and heating. Our rubbish was collected by a horse-drawn cart and the bread delivered from Chandler's, the bakers. They also brought our milk and newspapers.

Charlie Bifield

Church Lane

Four hundred yards up Church Lane there was a little wooden cottage with a thatched roof and we used to call it Goldilocks and the Three Bears, because it was so quaint. It didn't have inside doors and seemed to be covered in black tar or something. Mr and Mrs Ayres lived there with their two sons. Later the cottage was burned down. The Burtons, the Argents and the Fitches used to live in the lane too and their cottages were owned by the Vellacotts. Dick Fitch had no children – he used to work on the farm as a ploughman, and his two horses were his life. Mr Argent worked on the farm and Mr Burton was the milkman at Willows farm – he did the milking and such. Mr Vellacott, the farmer, was a very religious man and allowed no smoking. Naturally the farm hands would have a crafty smoke when they were hoeing or working in the fields but if any of them were caught – he'd sack them immediately.

Stanley Byford

Aunty Annie's shop

I first visited Rainham in 1929. Having left the bus, my grandmother and I walked along Upminster Road South, past the rows of Victorian cottages to my Auntie Annie's shop, (A. & R. Smith, newsagents, tobacconists and confectioners.) The shop was on a corner at the right-hand side with a tall wooden fence surrounding the back yard. My aunt ran the shop while Uncle Ray worked elsewhere and

I was to stay for a few weeks during my school holidays. I was given a room overlooking the road and, by kneeling on the window seat, could watch the traffic. Milk was delivered directly into jugs held by housewives, from the churn carried on a horse-drawn milk float. An old open motor truck carried sacks of coal, which were humped into the houses. There were motorcycles with sidecars, delivery vans – some horse-drawn, and people on bicycles. On the opposite side of the road there was a row of beautiful chestnut trees in full bloom. They lined an open sports field behind a wooden fence and I'd watch matches taking place between local teams from my bedroom window. One day my uncle bought me a 'Sno-fuit,' which was a triangular stick of fruit-flavoured frozen ice wrapped in cardboard. It cost a penny and was bought from a Walls' salesman who rode a tricycle with a large, square box on the front. It invited people to, 'stop me and buy one'.

Robert R. Brown

Robert R. Brown.

Float used by Residents' Assocation at election time. 'Keep Rainham and Wennington in the Swim'.

Procession floats

When the Residents' Association put up for re-election we themed our floats as to the current or next project we had in mind. For instance, in 1968 when we were involved with the swimming pool plan, our theme was, 'Keep Rainham in the Swim.' This was part of our street procession the Saturday before polling day. I must admit it's very satisfying to look around and see all the things I was involved with from the beginning.

Don Poole

War Memorial

When I was a child, I'd see two or three old ladies passing by the post office with boxes on wheels, going down to the 'shoot' to see what they could find. The hotels used to dump unwanted goods there – and knives and forks etc. were there for the taking. I watched the War Memorial being built – I can remember the big ceremony when it was officially unveiled by the Lord Lieutenant of Essex.

Ruth Daws

Marriage in the thirties

My husband was the brother of a friend of mine, and we got married in Rainham church in 1929. I had a white wedding with six bridesmaids dressed in pale green. Our first house was No. 12, Melville Road and I lived there for eleven years. My daughter was born in 1933 and as it was before the National Health Service, I had to pay for the nurse and doctor who attended my confinement. I joined a little club to pay for it. You'd never be allowed to do any washing on Sunday in those days and I've known my father-in-law take a pair of stockings off the line and bring them in. We moved to Eastwood Drive in 1939.

Vi Watts

Wennington Hut

Wennington Hut was built for the parishioners and they wanted to play bingo and whist and the like, but the Revd Norton wouldn't allow it because it was on ground belonging to the church. He had a big house built for himself by the fire station.

Stanley Byford

Taxidermy

My mother was born at No. 75, Wennington Road and my grandfather was a coal porter. One of my uncles was reputed to have been a long distance runner but was also interested in taxidermy. One room in the house had

an entire wall dedicated to stuffed birds and animals. He was my uncle Alec and was the last of our family to live there.

George Barrett

Open views

I remember when there were three shops in Wennington but there aren't any now. I can recall when there was nothing from Ferry Lane to the brook at Wennington – there wasn't a house on the marshes side. I think they started building in about 1927.

Grace Dalton

Early fire brigade

Further along from Rose Cottages towards the village there was a blacksmith's shop, and then the school, and after that a building where they kept the fire engine. It was

Open views across farmland at Wennington.

called the Merryweather. We didn't have a fire brigade at that time but if there was a fire, the volunteers from the community used to be called together. They'd come running along the road in their tin helmets, ready to get on the fire engine.

Edna Harris (*née* Hawes)

Alf Hazell

Alf Hazell who ran the post office was really nice – you could go in there and get ten Woodbines on the 'book' and not pay until Friday. If you were going on holiday, he'd pay the Family Allowance weeks in advance. He enjoyed a chat and if you had time he'd make you a cup of tea. There were about twenty stools in the shop for people who wanted a sit down. My wife used to make him a huge bread pudding.

Peter Smith

Crusty rolls

I remember the crusty rolls Dad used to bring in for breakfast on Saturday. He loved a piece of fresh haddock and would buy it from Jim's Fish Shop in the Wennington Road. I'd be at the table, waiting anxiously for him to break me off a piece of his fish to put in my roll.

Ann Waller (*née* Chandler)

New life in the country

Wennington was a wonderful place for the children to grow up in – there was no fear of accidents. They'd play on the marshes at the back of the house and from time to time I'd go to a bedroom window just to check on them and make sure they were all right – but I had no real fears that anything would happen to them. I used to buy my groceries from Byford's when I first moved in. Mr Cutmore sold groceries too.

Mr Hazell had the post office and it was right by the bus stop – so if it was raining

you could wait for the bus in his shop and pass the time having a gossip. And the baker used to call regularly as did the greengrocer, fishmonger and the milkman of course, so we were very well served in those days. The Green Line bus ran through here then, so we weren't isolated, and there was the local bus that ran about every half hour – although we did a lot of walking in those days. We'd walk to Rainham where they had some very nice shops. We were also lucky in that when Kent View was built and we moved in, we knew the rest of the group so had ready-made friends. We got to know the rest of the people in the village and were made very welcome.

Elizabeth Wiegold

Granny Byford

My granny Byford lived in a cottage at Coldharbour and my dad was born there in the 1800s, but later granny moved to Laundry Cottages. There was a Mr Jones at Laundry Cottages, he had a cine camera and he used to invite me in to watch films with his two boys.

Stanley Byford

Card sharps

My father used to work as an interpreter for Jurgens Van Den Bergh, the margarine factory in Thurrock. He learned to speak German when he was a prisoner in the First World War. He'd travel to work by train and laugh as he recalled the guards coming round quite regularly, warning passengers there were card sharps on board. 'Card sharps aboard, card sharps aboard', they'd call out.

George Barrett

Looking back

Burr's the shoe shop was in Upminster Road South and further along there was a double-fronted house which was turned into the post office that was run by Mr Holmes. Mr Durley used to come round with his milk cart, and Price's delivered the bread by horse and cart, as did Bubble Deeks with the vegetables. Opposite the church where the library now stands there used to be an abattoir – it was run by a Mr Mayhew – but I didn't ever go in there.

Edna Harris (*née* Hawes)

Randall Court

I enjoyed my years in Wennington but when I lost my husband I didn't want to be on my own, so decided to move into sheltered housing about twenty-five years ago. I saw Randall Court being built in Rainham and liked it. There are people to talk to here and we play bingo and hoy, and people visit me, so I'm very content.

Dot Barrack

Happiness

Rainham had a very close-knit community and was a wonderful place to grow up in but after marrying in Rainham church we moved away.

Edna Harris (*née* Hawes)

The Cherry Tree pub

There was little to keep anybody at home on Saturday evenings when I was a child so my parents would walk to the Cherry Tree pub and I'd wait outside for them, having been given an arrowroot biscuit and a glass of lemonade. I'd press my nose against the frosted glass, willing them to take me home.

Derek Chaproniere

The Whitbys

My mother was Daisy Whitby – she became Daisy Parker after her marriage. She lived at Ferry Point as a child, before my nan and granddad took the family to live at No. 10, Bell Terrace. At that time the rent was 11s 6d a week. Bell Terrace was renamed Bridge Road in 1962 but was always known to locals as Flood Row, as the houses were flooded so often. By 1964 the weekly rent was 18s 9d.

The old Three Crowns pub at Rainham Creek, *c*.1910.

Rainham church.

Granddad was the first policeman in Rainham, his area stretching from Rainham Ferry to Dagenham. He covered his route by bicycle. The name of Jack Whitby appears on the Rainham War Memorial and he's an uncle of ours who was killed in action when he was fourteen. When Mum and Dad married they went to live next door to my grandparents. Mum and Dad had six children and we were all born at No. 11, Bridge Road, squeezing into a two-up, two-down house. I was the third of six children and the family continued to live there until the houses were pulled down. Our lives were often disrupted by the floods. In 1967 the family moved to Christchurch Avenue at the Cherry Tree. Dad had just died and after all that hardship in Flood Row, Mum only lived for another eighteen months. A lot of people wouldn't leave when we were given notice to quit Bridge Road as they'd made their houses look nice and were used to living there. Although we didn't know it at the time,

Tesco had bought the land and I'm fond of telling people that the store's deli counter is built on the ground where our house used to be. Tesco opened in January 1991.

Jenny Scudder (*née* Parker)

Lollipop man

Mr Cunnington was the first lollipop man in Rainham and was known as Uncle Bert.

Ruth Daws

Ferry

In the early 1900s Old Ted Walls' father used to run a ferry from the Three Crowns over to Erith.

Peter Gleeson

Armed guard

There was a firing range on the right-hand side of Ferry Lane as well, between Bendy

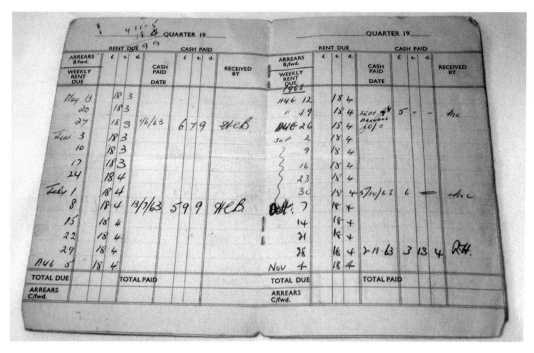

Bridge Road rent book.

Hook and the Half Way House. They'd fire right across the road, so there was an armed guard to stop people in case they got hurt.

Madeline Fatharly

Finding babies

My mother used to tell tales of finding dead babies on the beach at Ferry Point in the old days, and if you took them to the police station you'd get 2s 6d; we assumed they'd been thrown overboard by passing boats because the river was very busy then.

Jenny Scudder

Retirement

Although Dad retired and left the pub at sixty-five he didn't get a pension until he was seventy as he'd been self-employed. That's how it was in 1936. We went to live in Wilfred Avenue where some new houses were being built. I used to deliver the church magazine so knew a lot of people who lived around there.

Charlie Bifield

Bell's bazaar

I was born in 1925 and they had some lovely shops in Rainham when I was a child – I used to love rummaging around Bell's Bazaar which sold all sorts of knick-knacks.

Vera Dawson (*née* Payne)

Fire station

A new fire station was opened at Wennington on 10 August 1962 and was absorbed into the enlarged London Fire Brigade on 1 April 1965. The station stands on the site of a former button factory.

Alan Painter

The Swifts

Mr and Mrs Swift worked for Murex and had a bungalow on Frog Island – they'd row over to the pub at high tide. Sometimes they'd play cards and miss the tide back so would have to wait for the next one.

Charlie Bifield

Getting married

Dad wouldn't allow us to get married until we had somewhere to live because he used to say, 'you don't buy a bird without providing it with a cage.'

Vera Dawson (*née* Payne)

Egg custard

There was old Mrs Clarke living in Wennington in the old days, and if she heard anybody was ill, she used to make them an egg custard.

Peter Gleeson

Motorcycle

I bought a BSA bike when I left school in the 1930s – or rather my dad bought it and I repaid him at 2s 6d per week – that was a lot of money in those days.

Stanley Byford

Local doctor

When I was a child, the doctor in Rainham was Dr Edward Danaher and his house was at the top of Melville Road. When he retired, Dr Harry Danaher took over; I think the house was called The Chestnuts.

Ruth Daws

The 'glow'

I wouldn't go to sleep until I'd seen my 'glow' when I was a child. This was when they opened the furnace at Murex and all the molten metal used to give off this lovely yellow, orange and golden glow that lit up the sky.

Kay Knight

Erith

When we lived in the pub at Ferry Point, our previous neighbours used to row across the river to visit us from Erith. Sometimes I think the husband was a bit the worse for wear for the return journey, but he seemed to manage to get back OK.

Charlie Bifield

Lenthorpe

Lenthorpe is the big house opposite Kent View, a scrap metal man used to live there and then he moved on and it was turned into flats.

Peter Gleeson

Sandals

On one occasion I bought a pair of sandals for 2s 6d – that would have been in about 1930.

Grace Dalton

Barratt-Lennards

A lot of the property around here used to belong to Barratt-Lennards who owned Belhus Park. The Lennard Arms is named after them.

Peter Gleeson

Weighing the babies

They used to weigh the babies in the church hall because I can remember Mum taking my baby brother there, and I was five when he was born in 1930.

Vera Dawson (*née* Payne)

Bikes

Outside the Byford café you'd see loads of bikes – they belonged to the farm workers.

Peter Smith

Telephones

There were very few telephones when we lived in the Three Crowns – our number was Rainham 32. The telephone exchange was in Melville Road.

Charlie Bifield

Carefree days, Wennington folk, 1937.

Other local titles published by Tempus

Barking and Dagenham
GAVIN SMITH

Barking and Dagenham have been sister communities on the Thames shore from Saxon times but the modern communities we know today began to take shape with the arrival of the Ford Company and the rapid growth of its manufacturing plant at Dagenham. This collection of old photographs illustrates many of the changes that have taken place and will appeal to all who live and work in the area.

0 7524 0739 2

Memories of Epping
CLARE BASTER

The market town of Epping has seen much expansion and a great many changes in its long history. Recollections of times past are recorded here along with over 100 archive photographs, many from private and unique collections. *Memories of Epping* will take the reader on a nostalgic journey into the past of this fascinating part of Essex and will delight all those who want to know more about the area.

0 7524 3453 5

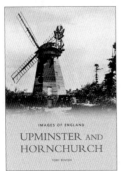

Upminster and Hornchurch
TONY BENTON

This selection of over 200 archive photographs of Upminster and Hornchurch brings to life the early decades of the twentieth century. The images range from shopping parades to children in their classrooms, Upminster's well-remembered May Festival and reflections on the 1914–18 war period in Hornchurch, when Grey Towers Mansion became a military camp and convalescent hospital.

0 7524 3206 0

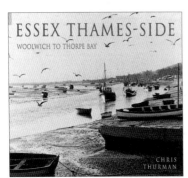

Essex Thames-side: Woolwich to Thorpe Bay
CHRIS THURMAN

Chris Thurman takes the reader on a tour of the Thames from Woolwich to Thorpe Bay on the Essex side of the river. From the futuristic sight of the Thames Barrier to sleepy Thorpe Bay, from unloading in the docks at Tilbury to cockling at Leigh on Sea, from Dagenham to Southend, the changing landscape of Essex Thames-side is photographed over the past forty years in this stunning collection of images.

0 7524 3232 X

If you are interested in purchasing other books published by Tempus, or in case you have difficulty finding any Tempus books in your local bookshop, you can also place orders directly through our website

www.tempus-publishing.com